The Kybalion, The Tablet of Hermes & The Emerald Tablets of Thoth:

Complete Hermetic Wisdom of Ancient Egypt, Atlantis, and Hermes Trismegistus

The Tablet of Hermes by Hermes Trismegistus

Translated by Anonymous

Emerald Tablets of Thoth Translated and Interpreted by Maurice Dorreal

The Kybalion by Three Initiates

The Kybalion, The Tablet of Hermes & The Emerald Tablets of Thoth:

Complete Hermetic Wisdom of Ancient Egypt, Atlantis, and Hermes Trismegistus

The Tablet of Hermes by Hermes Trismegistus

Translated by Anonymous

Emerald Tablets of Thoth Translated and Interpreted by Maurice Dorreal

The Kybalion by Three Initiates

All rights reserved.

Printed in the United States of America. No part of this book may be used or reproduced in any manner whatsoever without written permission except in the case of brief quotations embodied in critical articles and reviews.

Fifth Estate Publishing, Blountsville, AL 35031

Printed on acid-free paper

Library of Congress Control No:

ISBN: 978-1958450260

Fifth Estate, 2025

TABLE OF CONTENTS

THE FUSION OF THOTH AND HERMES	1
ORIGINS OF THE TABLET	5
CONNECTING THE KYBALION & TABLET OF HERMES	7
THE TABLET OF HERMES	9
THE EMERALD TABLETS OF THOTH	
PREFACE	11
INTRODUCTION	15
TABLET I : The History of Thoth, The Atlantean	17
TABLET II : The Halls of Amenti	23
TABLET III: The Key of Wisdom	29
TABLET IV: The Space Born	35
TABLET V: The Dweller of Unal	40
TABLET VI : The Key of Magic	46
TABLET VII : The Seven Lords	52
TABLET VIII: The Key of Mysteries	57
TABLET IX: The Key of Freedom of Space	63
TABLET X: The Key of Time	69
TABLET XI : The Key to Above and Below	75
TABLET XII : The Key of Prophecy	80
TABLET XIII : The Keys of Life and Death	85
SUPPLEMENTARY TABLET XIV: Atlantis	89
SUPPLEMENTARY TABLET XV: Secret of Secrets	95

THE KYBALION	**99**
INTRODUCTION	100
I. THE HERMETIC PHILOSOPHY	104
II. THE SEVEN HERMETIC PRINCIPLES	109
III. MENTAL TRANSMUTATION	120
IV. THE ALL	125
V. THE MENTAL UNIVERSE	131
VI. THE DIVINE PARADOX	137
VII. "THE ALL" IN ALL	146
VIII. PLANES OF CORRESPONDENCE	154
IX. VIBRATION	166
X. POLARITY	172
XI. RHYTHM	177
XII. CAUSATION	184
XIII. GENDER	190
XIV. MENTAL GENDER	196
XV. HERMETIC AXIOMS	206
FREE AUDIOBOOK ACCESS	**212**

The Fusion of Hermes and Thoth: Ancient Egypt to the Modern West

The figure of Hermes Trismegistus, "thrice-great Hermes," emerges from a rich history of religious and philosophical syncretism between the Greek messenger god Hermes and the Egyptian deity Thoth. This fusion came about through cultural and theological integration, showcasing the adaptability of religious traditions.

From approximately the 7th to the 4th centuries BCE, Greek traders and mercenaries established communities within the Nile Delta. These Greek settlers, practicing interpretatio graeca, the practice of equating foreign deities with familiar ones, recognized significant overlaps between Hermes and Thoth. Both gods presided over writing, magic, and psychopomp (soul guiding) duties. Thus, Greeks began to identify Thoth explicitly as "Egyptian Hermes," an identification attested by ancient historians like Herodotus and various papyri from the period (journals.uchicago.edu).

Under Ptolemaic rule (332–30 BCE), a concerted effort toward cultural integration intensified. The Egyptian city Khmunu, a major cult center for Thoth, was renamed Hermopolis Magna, literally "City of Hermes." Bilingual inscriptions and statues from this era explicitly reference the merged deity Hermes-Thoth, epitomized in artifacts such as the marble head housed in the Metropolitan Museum, complete with inscriptions articulating combined worship practices (metmuseum.org).

In the vibrant intellectual milieu of Alexandria during the early Roman Empire (1st–3rd centuries CE), Hermes Trismegistus crystallized into a legendary figure embodying both Egyptian and Greek wisdom. Priestly authors crafted texts, notably the Corpus Hermeticum and the enigmatic Emerald Tablet, in which Hermes

The Kybalion, The Tablet of Hermes, & The Emerald Tablets

Trismegistus spoke Greek but conveyed distinctly Egyptian philosophical teachings. In these texts, Hermes is depicted as both "lord of logos" and "scribe of the gods," directly reflecting the combined attributes of Hermes and Thoth (britannica.com).

The 8th to 10th centuries witnessed another wave of Hermes-Thoth adaptation as Greek scientific and philosophical texts entered the Arabic intellectual world. Hermes Trismegistus was equated with the prophet Idrīs and revered as a source of alchemical knowledge. Arabic translations of the Emerald Tablet proliferated, embedding Hermes deeply into Islamic alchemical traditions. Medieval Islamic scholars developed elaborate biographies of "The Three Hermeses," cementing Hermes' multifaceted identity as prophet, philosopher, and astronomer.

With the translation of Arabic and Greek Hermetic texts into Latin during the 12th to 17th centuries, Hermes Trismegistus entered European intellectual thought. Marsilio Ficino's 1463 Latin translation of the Corpus Hermeticum elevated Hermes to a sage predating Plato and paralleling Moses. Ficino positioned Hermetic wisdom as prisca theologia, an ancient theology reconciling Christian and pre-Christian wisdom, spurring an enduring Renaissance of occultism and philosophy.

In the 19th and 20th centuries, occult revivals, spiritualist movements, and groups like the Golden Dawn significantly popularized Hermes Trismegistus. Influential texts such as The Kybalion (1908) and Maurice Doreal's Emerald Tablets (1940s) reinterpreted Hermetic teachings, transforming ancient esoteric doctrines into accessible, self-help philosophies. These works explicitly invoked Hermes-Thoth, preserving the historical fusion while adapting it for contemporary spiritual seekers. Doreal's interpretation goes a step further, implying a fourth incarnation of

Fusion of Thoth and Hermes

the deity as an Atlantean king, Thoth the Atlantean. The evolution of Thoth can be visualized as such:

Thoth, Egyptian God of Wisdom →

Between 700 and 400 BC Greeks equate Thoth to their messenger god, Hermes (the second incarnation.) →

From the 3rd century BC to 1st century BC a hub of Thoth cultist, the city of Khmunu, is renamed after Hermes and the melding of these two gods accelerates→

By the first century CE, Hermes Trismegistus is solidified as a unique entity with scribes creating texts attributed to his teachings. This is the third incarnation (Thrice Great Hermes)→

In 1925 Maurice Doreal claims to have received a vision from the god Thoth, reimagined as an Atlantean king. This sparked the best selling translation released in the 1900s and symbolizes a fourth incarnation - The king of Atlantis.

Conclusion

The merging of Hermes and Thoth into Hermes Trismegistus was neither accidental nor singular. Instead, it represents a continual 2,500-year intercultural exchange. This fusion reflects the shared characteristics of Hermes and Thoth, such as their roles in magic, writing, and guiding souls, which enabled their seamless combination into one transcultural sage. The combined entities have notably paralleled other key figures in other religions such as Enoch from Jewish culture and Idris from Islam. The reemergence of popularity surrounding this text may signify a continuing evolution past the fourth incarnation seen in 1925. Hermes Trismegistus thus exemplifies the flexibility and resilience of religious and philosophical traditions, persisting as a central figure in global spiritual thought.

Origins of the Tablet

When modern readers pick up Maurice Doreal's *Emerald Tablets of Thoth the Atlantean* (first circulated in the 1930s), they often assume it is the same text that medieval alchemists revered as the "Emerald Tablet of Hermes." In fact, Doreal's work is a twentieth-century occult expansion that shares little more than the name and the mystique of green stone. The authentic *Tabula Smaragdina*, a terse set of thirteen aphorisms known from Arabic and Latin manuscripts, has a far older and much more tangled history.

The historical Tablet first reached medieval Europe inside the pseudo-Aristotelian *Secretum Secretorum*, itself a Latin translation (c. 1140–1243) of the Arabic *Kitāb Sirr al-Asrār*, a handbook of statecraft for kings. Even earlier Arabic witnesses survive: one version appears in the *Kitāb Ustuqus al-Uss al-Thānī* attributed to the eighth-century alchemist Jābir ibn Ḥayyān, while another is appended to the *Kitāb Sirr al-Khalīqa wa-Ṣan'at al-Ṭabī'a* (often dated no later than the reign of the 'Abbāsid caliph al-Ma'mūn, 813-833 CE). Scholars have noted parallels between these Arabic treatises and earlier Syriac and Greek writings, yet none of those antecedents contains the Tablet itself, leaving its ultimate origin obscure—possibilities range from Hellenistic Egypt to farther eastward, even China (Needham 1980; Holmyard 1957).

What unites all pre-modern versions is brevity and philosophical focus: a few hundred words on cosmic correspondence ("as above, so below"), the generation of the elements, and the perfection of the *One Thing*. Doreal, by contrast, unfolds fifteen lengthy chapters of Atlantean lore, astral travel, and millennial prophecy enlivened by modern Theosophical and science-fiction motifs. Whereas the medieval Tablet is documented in multiple manuscript families

The Kybalion, The Tablet of Hermes, & The Emerald Tablets

and critical editions (e.g., Ruska 1926), Doreal's source remains undocumented: he claimed to have translated emerald-green stone tablets housed in the Great Pyramid, yet no independent witness has ever seen them.

In short, the historical Emerald Tablet is a late-antique Hermetic fragment that entered Western thought through Arabic science and Latin alchemy; Doreal's *Emerald Tablets* are a modern esoteric narrative that repurposes the Tablet's aura to tell an entirely new story. Recognizing this distinction is essential before comparing the teachings each text offers, or judging the authority each can rightly claim.

Connection of The Kybalion and The Tablet of Hermes

Modern scholars regard *The Kybalion* (1908) primarily as a product of the early-20th-century American New Thought movement rather than as a genuine continuation of ancient Hermetic literature. Its central maxim, "As above, so below," links it thematically to the older Emerald Tablet (Tabula Smaragdina) of Hermes, yet this connection arises from appropriation and creative reinterpretation rather than direct textual lineage. Published initially by the Yogi Publication Society in Chicago, *The Kybalion* is now universally attributed to William Walker Atkinson, who wrote under the pseudonym "Three Initiates." Philip Deslippe's research conclusively identifies Atkinson as the author, grounding this identification in biographical and textual evidence. Atkinson's work embodies core New Thought principles, emphasizing mental causation, autosuggestion, and pragmatic self-help rather than the theurgical or devotional practices typical of ancient Hermetism. Nicholas Chapel has shown that the famous "Seven Hermetic Principles" outlined in *The Kybalion* parallel concepts already prevalent in late 19th-century New Thought literature. Atkinson invoked the legendary Hermes Trismegistus to lend authority and ancient prestige to his synthesis, despite the absence of any historical basis for the title "Kybalion" or its seven principles within genuine classical Hermetic texts.

The Emerald Tablet itself first appears historically in an Arabic encyclopedic work from the late 8th or early 9th century. Its key phrase—"That which is above is like that which is below"—occurs consistently in medieval versions. Julius Ruska's definitive 1926 scholarly examination revealed that the Tablet had no genuine ancient Egyptian origins, countering Renaissance claims of its antiquity. Brian P. Copenhaver's 1992 edition provides the modern scholarly framework for understanding and evaluating Hermetic literature, clarifying the Tablet's historical development and transmission.

When comparing *The Kybalion* to the Emerald Tablet, scholars note specific but limited points of appropriation. Atkinson directly borrowed the Tablet's principle of correspondence ("As above, so below") from 19th-century occult handbooks rather than original sources. Additionally, Atkinson transformed the alchemical symbolism of the Tablet into a psychological metaphor of "mental transmutation," shifting the focus from laboratory alchemy to New Thought's emphasis on mental empowerment. The idea of a universal mind, or "The All," present in *The Kybalion*, significantly expands upon ideas only faintly suggested in the Emerald Tablet, leaning instead into later Hermetic concepts influenced by Platonic and Stoic traditions.

Scholars express skepticism regarding any deep historical connection between the two texts due to selective borrowing, doctrinal differences, and a significant temporal gap of approximately 1,100 years separating the Tablet's earliest Arabic sources from Atkinson's 20th-century creation. Christian H. Bull situates both works in distinct historical contexts, distinguishing between authentic late-antique Hermetism and the 19th-century occult revival that mediated Atkinson's interpretation. Overall, scholarly consensus identifies *The Kybalion* as a modern reinterpretation of Hermetic motifs framed strategically as ancient wisdom, emphasizing that its continuity with authentic Hermetic traditions is a creative construct rather than a genuine historical transmission. This phenomenon reflects a broader pattern in Western esoteric traditions, where contemporary spiritual seekers re-stage ancient symbols and motifs to meet modern spiritual and philosophical needs, producing works that appear ancient but whose true origins are demonstrably modern.

The Tablet of Hermes (from the German of Ruska, translated by 'Anonymous').

0) Here is that which the priest Sagijus of Nabulus has dictated concerning the entrance of Balinas into the hidden chamber... After my entrance into the chamber, where the talisman was set up, I came up to an old man sitting on a golden throne, who was holding an emerald tablet in one hand.

And behold the following in Syriac, the primordial language, was written thereon:

1) Here (is) a true explanation, concerning which there can be no doubt.

2) It attests: The above from the below, and the below from the above −the work of the miracle of the One.

3) And things have been from this primal substance through a single act. How wonderful is this work! It is the main (principle) of the world and is its maintainer.

4) Its father is the sun and its mother the moon; the

5) wind has borne it in its body, and the earth has nourished it.

6) the father of talismen and the protector of miracles (other translations read "the father of all wonders" or "the father of all things")

6a) whose powers are perfect, and whose lights are confirmed (?), (Other translations read "It is power perfected")

7) a fire that becomes earth.

7a) Separate the earth from the fire, so you will attain the subtle as more inherent than the gross, with care and sagacity.

The Tablet of Hermes

8) It rises from earth to heaven, so as to draw the lights of the heights to itself, and descends to the earth; thus within it are the forces of the above and the below;

9) because the light of lights within it, thus does the darkness flee before it.

10) The force of forces, which overcomes every subtle thing and penetrates into everything gross.

11) The structure of the microcosm is in accordance with the structure of the macrocosm.

12) And accordingly proceed the knowledgeable.

13) And to this aspired Hermes, who was threefold graced with wisdom.

14) And this is his last book, which he concealed in the chamber.

[Anon 1985: 24–5]

PREFACE to the original The Emerald Tablets of Thoth the Atlantean by Doreal

The history of the tablets translated in the following pages is strange and beyond the belief of modern scientists. Their antiquity is stupendous, dating back some 36,000 years B.C. The writer is Thoth, an Atlantean Priest-King, who founded a colony in ancient Egypt after the sinking of the mother country.

He was the builder of the Great Pyramid of Giza, erroneously attributed to Cheops. (See The Great Pyramid by Doreal.) In it he incorporated his knowledge of the ancient wisdom and also securely secreted records and instruments of ancient Atlantis.

For some 16,000 years, he ruled the ancient race of Egypt, from approximately 50,000 B.C. to 36.000 B.C. At that time, the ancient barbarous race among which he and his followers had settled had been raised to a high degree of civilization.

Thoth was an immortal, that is, he had conquered death, passing only when he willed and even then not through death. His vast wisdom made him ruler over the various Atlantean colonies, including the ones in South and Central America.

When the time came for him to leave Egypt, he erected the Great Pyramid over the entrance to the Great Halls of Amenti, placed in it his records, and appointed guards for his secrets from among the highest of his people.

In later times, the descendants of these guards became the pyramid priests, by which Thoth was deified as the God of Wisdom, The Recorder, by those in the age of darkness which followed his

The Emerald Tablets

passing. In legend, the halls of Amenti became the underworld, the Halls of the Gods, where the soul passed after death for judgment.

During later ages, the ego of Thoth passed into the bodies of men in the manner described in the tablets. As such, he incarnated three times, in his last being known as Hermes, the thrice-born. In this incarnation, he left the writings known to modern occultists as the Emerald Tablets, a later and far lesser exposition of the ancient mysteries.

The tablets translated in this work are ten which were left in the Great Pyramid in the custody of the pyramid priests. The ten are divided into thirteen parts for the sake of convenience.

The last two are so great and far-reaching in their import that at present it is forbidden to release them to the world at large. However, in those contained herein are secrets which will prove of inestimable value to the serious student.

They should be read, not once, but a hundred times for only thus can the true meaning be revealed. A casual reading will give glimpses of beauty, but more intensive study will oven avenues of wisdom to the seeker.

But now a word as to how these mighty secrets came to be revealed to modern man after being hidden so long.

Some thirteen hundred years B.C., Egypt, the ancient Khem, was in turmoil and many delegations of priests were sent to other parts of the world. Among these were some of the pyramid priests who carried with them the Emerald Tablets as a talisman by which they could exercise authority over the less advanced priest-craft of races descended from other Atlantean colonies.

Preface

The tablets were understood from legend to give the bearer authority from Thoth.

The particular group of priests bearing the tablets emigrated to South America where they found a flourishing race, the Mayas who remembered much of the ancient wisdom.

Among these, the priests settled and remained. In the tenth century, the Mayas had thoroughly settled the Yucatan, and the tablets were placed beneath the altar of one of the great temples of the Sun God.

After the conquest of the Mayas by the Spaniards, the cities were abandoned and the treasures of the temples forgotten.

It should be understood that the Great Pyramid of Egypt has been and still is a temple of initiation into the mysteries. Jesus, Solomon, Apollonius and others were initiated there.

The writer (who has a connection with the Great White Lodge which also works through the pyramid priesthood) was instructed to recover and return to the Great Pyramid the ancient tablets.

This, after adventures which need not be detailed here, was accomplished. Before returning them, he was given permission to translate and retain a copy of the wisdom engraved on the tablets.

This was done in 1925 and only now has permission been given for part to be published. It is expected that many will scoff. Yet the true student will read between the lines and gain wisdom.

If the light is in you, the light which is engraved in these tablets will respond.

Now, a word as to the material aspect of the tablets.

The Emerald Tablets

They consist of twelve tablets of emerald green, formed from a substance created through alchemical transmutation.

They are imperishable, resistant to all elements and substances. In effect, the atomic and cellular structure is fixed, no change ever taking place.

In this respect, they violate the material law of ionization.

Upon them are engraved characters in the ancient Atlantean language: characters which respond to attuned thought waves, releasing the associated mental vibration in the mind of the reader.

The tablets are fastened together with hoops of golden-colored alloy suspended from a rod of the same material. So much for the material appearance.

The wisdom contained therein is the foundation of the ancient mysteries. And for the one who reads with open eyes and mind, his wisdom shall be increased a hundred-fold.

Read. Believe or not, but read. And the vibration found therein will awaken a response in your soul.

Doreal

INTRODUCTION to the original An Interpretation of the Emerald Tablets by Doreal

In the following pages, I will reveal some of the mysteries which as yet have only been touched upon lightly either by myself or other teachers or students of truth.

Man's search for understanding of the laws which regulate his life has been unending, yet always just beyond the veil which shields the higher planes from material man's vision the truth has existed, ready to be assimilated by those who enlarge their vision by turning inward, not outward, in their search.

In the silence of material senses lies the key to the unveiling of wisdom. He who talks does not know; he who knows does not talk. The highest knowledge is unutterable, for it exists as an entity in lanes which transcend all material words or symbols.

All symbols are but keys to doors leading to truths, and many times the door is not opened because the key seems so great that the things which are beyond it are not visible. If we can understand that all keys, all material symbols are manifestations, are but extensions of a great law and truth, we will begin to develop the vision which will enable us to penetrate beyond the veil.

All things in all universes move according to law, and the law which regulates the movement of the planets is no more immutable than the law which regulates the material expressions of man.

One of the greatest of all Cosmic Laws is that which is responsible for the formation of man as a material being. The great aim of the mystery schools of all ages has been to reveal the workings of the Law which connect man the material and man the spiritual.

The Emerald Tablets

The connecting link between the material man and the spiritual man is the intellectual man, for the mind partakes of both the material and immaterial qualities. The aspirant for higher knowledge must develop the intellectual side of his nature and so strengthen his will that is able to concentrate all powers of his being on and in the plane he desires.

The great search for light, life and love only begins on the material plane. Carried to its ultimate, its final goal is complete oneness with the universal consciousness. The foundation in the material is the first step; then comes the higher goal of spiritual attainment.

In the following pages, I will give an interpretation of the Emerald Tablets and their secret, hidden and esoteric meanings. Concealed in the words of Thoth are many meanings that do not appear on the surface. Light of knowledge brought to bear upon the Tablets will open many new fields for thought.

"Read and be wise" but only if the light of your own consciousness awakens the deep-seated understanding which is an inherent quality of the soul.

Doreal

EMERALD TABLET I
The History of Thoth, The Atlantean

I, Thoth, the Atlantean, master of mysteries, keeper of records, mighty king, magician, living from generation to generation, being about to pass into the Halls of Amenti, set down for the guidance of those that are to come after, these records of the mighty wisdom of Great Atlantis.

In the great city of Keor on the island of Undal in a time far past, I began this incarnation. Not as the little men of the present age did the mighty ones of Atlantis live and die, but rather from aeon to aeon did they renew their life in the Halls of Amenti where the river of life flows eternally onward.

A hundred times ten have I descended the dark way that led into light, and as many times have I ascended from the darkness into the light, my strength and power renewed.

Now for a time I descend, and the men of Khem shall know me no more. But in a time yet unborn will I rise again, mighty and potent, requiring an accounting of those left behind me.

Then beware, O men of Khem, if ye have falsely betrayed my teaching, for I shall cast ye down from your high estate into the darkness of the caves from whence ye came. Betray not my secrets to the men of the North or the men of the South lest my curse fall upon ye.

Remember and heed my words, for surely will I return again and require of thee that which ye guard. Aye, even from beyond time and from beyond death will I return, rewarding or punishing as ye have requited your trust.

The Emerald Tablets

Great were my people in the ancient days, great beyond the conception of the little people now around me; knowing the wisdom of old, seeking far within the heart of infinity knowledge that belonged to Earth's youth.

Wise were we with the wisdom of the Children of Light who dwelt among us. Strong were we with the power drawn from the eternal fire.

And of all these, greatest among the children of men was my father, Thotme, keeper of the great temple, link between the Children of Light who dwelt within the temple and the races of men who inhabited the ten islands.

Mouthpiece, after the three, of the Dweller of Unal, speaking to the Kings with the voice that must be obeyed.

Grew I there from a child into manhood, being taught by my father the elder mysteries, until in time there grew within the fire of wisdom, until it burst into a consuming flame. Naught desired I but the attainment of wisdom.

Until on a great day the command came from the Dweller of the Temple that I be brought before him. Few there were among the children of men who had looked upon that mighty face and lived, for not as the sons of men are the Children of Light when they are not incarnate in a physical body.

Chosen was I from the sons of men, taught by the Dweller so that his purposes might be fulfilled, purposes yet unborn in the womb of time.

Long ages I dwelt in the Temple, learning ever and yet ever more wisdom, until I, too, approached the light emitted from the great fire.

The History of Thoth, The Atlantean

Taught me he, the path to Amenti, the underworld where the great king sits upon his throne of might. Deep I bowed in homage before the Lords of Life and the Lords of Death, receiving as my gift the key of Life. Free was I of the Halls of Amenti, bound not by death to the circle of life. Far to the stars I journeyed until space and time became as naught.

Then having drunk deep of the cup of wisdom, I looked into the hearts of men and there found I greater mysteries and was glad. For only in the Search for Truth could my Soul be stilled and the flame within be quenched.

Down through the ages I lived, seeing those around me taste of the cup of death and return again in the light of life. Gradually from the Kingdoms of Atlantis passed waves of consciousness that had been one with me, only to be replaced by spawn of a lower star.

In obedience to the law, the word of the Master grew into flower. Downward into darkness turned the thoughts of the Atlanteans, until at last in his wrath arose from his Agwanti, the Dweller, (this word has no English equivalent; it means a state of detachment) speaking The Word, calling the power. Deep in Earth's heart, the sons of Amenti heard, and hearing, directed the changing of the flower of fire that burns eternally, changing and shifting, using the Logos, until that great fire changed its direction.

Over the world then broke the great waters, drowning and sinking, changing Earth's balance until only the Temple of Light was left standing on the great mountain on Undal still rising out of the water; some there were who were living, saved from the rush of the fountains.

Called to me then the Master, saying: "Gather ye together my people. Take them by the arts ye have learned of far across the waters, until ye reach the land of the hairy barbarians, dwelling in caves of the desert. Follow there the plan that ye know of."

Gathered I then my people and entered the great ship of the Master. Upward we rose into the morning. Dark beneath us lay the Temple. Suddenly over it rose the waters.

Vanished from Earth, until the time appointed, was the great Temple.

Fast we fled toward the sun of the morning, until beneath us lay the land of the children of Khem. Raging, they came with cudgels and spears lifted in anger seeking to slay and utterly destroy the Sons of Atlantis. Then raised I my staff and directed a ray of vibration, striking them still in their tracks as fragments of stone of the mountain.

Then spoke I to them in words calm and peaceful, telling them of the might of Atlantis, saying we were children of the Sun and its messengers. Cowed I them by my display of magicscience, until at my feet they grovelled, when I released them.

Long dwelt we in the land of Khem, long and yet long again. Until obeying the commands of the Master, who while sleeping yet lives eternally, I sent from me the Sons of

Atlantis, sent them in many directions, that from the womb of time wisdom might rise again in her children.

Long time dwelt I in the land of Khem, doing great works by the wisdom within me.

Upward grew into the light of knowledge the children of Khem, watered by the rains of my wisdom. Blasted I then a path to

The History of Thoth, The Atlantean

Amenti so that I might retain my powers, living from age to age a Sun of Atlantis, keeping the wisdom, preserving the records.

Great grew the sons of Khem, conquering the people around them, growing slowly upwards in Soul force.

Now for a time I go from among them into the dark halls of Amenti, deep in the halls of the Earth, before the Lords of the Powers, face to face once again with the Dweller.

Raised I high over the entrance, a doorway, a gateway leading down to Amenti. Few there would be with courage to dare it, few pass the portal to dark Amenti. Raised over the passage, I, a mighty pyramid, using the power that overcomes Earth force (gravity).

Deep and yet deeper placed I a force- house or chamber; from it carved I a circular passage reaching almost to the great summit. There in the apex, set I the crystal, sending the ray into the "Time-Space", drawing the force from out of the ether, concentrating upon the gateway to Amenti. (See The Great Pyramid by Doreal.)

Other chambers I built and left vacant to all seeming, yet hidden within them are the keys to Amenti. He who in courage would dare the dark realms, let him be purified first by long fasting. Lie in the sarcophagus of stone in my chamber.

Then to reveal I to him the great mysteries. Soon shall he follow to where I shall meet him, even in the darkness of Earth shall I meet him, I, Thoth, Lord of Wisdom, meet him and hold him and dwell with him always.

Built I the Great Pyramid, patterned after the pyramid of earth force, burning eternally so that it, too, might remain through the ages. In it, I built my knowledge of "Magic-Science" so that it might be here when again I return from Amenti. Aye, while I sleep in the Halls of Amenti, my Soul roaming free will incarnate, dwell among men in this form or another. (Hermes, thrice-born.)

Emissary on Earth am I of the Dweller, fulfilling his commands so man might be lifted. Now return I to the Halls of Amenti, leaving behind me some of my wisdom. Preserve ye and keep ye the command of the Dweller: Lift ever upwards your eyes toward the light. Surely in time, ye are one with the Master, surely by right ye are one with the Master, surely by right ye are one with the All.

Now I depart from ye. Know my commandments, keep them and be them, and I will be with you, helping and guiding you into the Light.

Now before me opens the portal. Go I down in the darkness of night.

EMERALD TABLET II
The Halls of Amenti

Deep in the Earth's heart lie the Halls of Amenti, far 'neath the islands of sunken Atlantis, Halls of the Dead and halls of the living, bathed in the fire of the infinite ALL.

Far in a past time, lost in the space time, the Children of Light looked down on the world. See the children of men in their bondage, bound by the force that came from beyond. Knew they that only by freedom from bondage could man ever rise from the Earth to the Sun. Down they descended and created bodies, taking the semblance of men as their own. The masters of everything said after their forming: "We are they who were formed from the space-dust, partaking of life from the infinite ALL; living in the world as children of men, like and yet unlike the children of men."

Then for a dwelling place, far 'neath the earth crust, blasted great spaces they by their power, spaces apart from the children of men. Surrounded them by forces and power, shielded from harm they the Halls of the Dead.

Side by side then, placed they other spaces, filled them with Life and with Light from above. Builded they then the Halls of Amenti, that they might dwell eternally there living with life to eternity's end.

Thirty and two were there of the children, sons of Light who had come among men, seeking to free from the bondage of darkness those who were bound by the force from beyond.

Deep in the Halls of Life grew a flower, flaming, expanding, driving backward the night. Placed in the center, a ray of great potence, Life giving, Light giving, filling with power all who came near it. Placed they around it thrones, two and thirty, places for each of the Children of Light, placed so that they were bathed in the radiance, filled with the Life from the eternal Light.

There time after time placed they their first created bodies so that they might be filled with the Spirit of Life. One hundred years out of each thousand must the Life-giving Light flame forth on their bodies. Quickening, awakening the Spirit of Life.

There in the circle from aeon to aeon, sit the Great Masters, living a life not known among men. There in the Halls of Life they lie sleeping; free flows their Soul through the bodies of men. Time after time, while their bodies lie sleeping, incarnate they in the bodies of men. Teaching and guiding onward and upward, out of the darkness into the Light.

There in the Hall of Life, filled with their wisdom, known not to the races of man, living forever 'neath the cold fire of life, sit the Children of Light. Times there are when they awaken, come from the depths to be lights among men, infinite they among finite.

He who by progress has grown from the darkness, lifted himself from the night into light, free is he made of the Halls of Amenti, free of the Flower of Light and of Life.

Guided he then, by wisdom and knowledge, passes from man, to the Master of Life.

There he may dwell as one with the Masters, free from the bonds of the darkness of night.

Seated within the flower of radiance sit seven Lords from the Space-Time above us, helping and guiding through infinite Wisdom, the pathway through time of the children of men. Mighty and strange, they, veiled with their power, silent, all-knowing, drawing the Life force, different yet one with the children of men.

Aye, different, and yet one with the Children of Light. Custodians and watchers of the force of man's bondage, ready to loose when the light has been reached. First and most mighty, sits the Veiled Presence, Lord of Lords, the infinite Nine, over the others from each Cosmic cycle, weighing and watching the progress of men.

Under HE, sit the Lords of the Cycles; Three, Four, Five, and Six, Seven, Eight, each with his mission, each with his power, guiding, directing the destiny of man.

There sit they, mighty and potent, free of all time and space. Not of this world they, yet akin to it, Elder Brothers they, of the children of men. Judging and weighing, they with their wisdom, watching the progress Light among men.

There before them was I led by the Dweller, watched him blend with ONE from above. Then from HE came forth a voice saying: "Great art thou, Thoth, among children of men. Free henceforth of the Halls of Amenti, Master of Life among children of men.

Taste not of death except as thou will it, drink thou of Life to Eternity's end. Henceforth forever is Life, thine for the taking. Henceforth is Death at the call of thy hand. Dwell here or leave here when thou desireth, free is Amenti to the Sun of man. Take thou up Life in what form thou desireth, Child of the Light that has grown among men. Choose thou thy work, for all souls must labor, never be free from the pathway of Light.

One step thou has gained on the long pathway upward, infinite now is the mountain of Light.

The Emerald Tablets

Each step thou taketh but heightens the mountain; all of thy progress but lengthens the goal. Approach ye ever the infinite Wisdom, ever before thee recedes the goal.

Free are ye made now of the Halls of Amenti to walk hand in hand with the Lords of the world, one in one purpose, working together, bringers of Light to the children of men."

Then from his throne came one of the Masters, taking my hand and leading me onward, through all the Halls of the deep hidden land. Led he me through the Halls of Amenti, showing the mysteries that are known not to man.

Through the dark passage, downward he led me into the Hall where sits the dark Death. Vast as space lay the great Hall before me, walled by darkness but yet filled with Light.

Before me arose a great throne of darkness, veiled on it seated a figure of night. Darker than darkness sat the great figure, dark with a darkness not of the night.

Before it then paused the Master, speaking The Word that brings about Life, saying: "Oh, master of darkness, guide of the way from Life unto Life, before thee I bring a Sun of the morning. Touch him not ever with the power of night. Call not his flame to the darkness of night. Know him, and see him, one of our brothers, lifted from darkness into the Light. Release thou his flame from its bondage, free let it flame through the darkness of night."

Raised then the hand of the figure, forth came a flame that grew clear and bright. Rolled back swiftly the curtain of darkness, unveiled the Hall from the darkness of night.

Then grew in the great space before me, flame after flame, from the veil of the night.

The Halls of Amenti

Uncounted millions leaped they before me, some flaming forth as flowers of fire. Others there were that shed a dim radiance, glowing but faintly from out of the night. Some there were that faded swiftly; others that grew from a small spark of light. Each surrounded by its dim veil of darkness, yet flaming with the light that could never be quenched. Coming and going like fireflies in springtime, filled they the space with Light and with Life.

Then spoke a voice, mighty and solemn, saying: "These are lights that are souls among men, growing and fading, existing forever, changing yet living, through death into life. When they have bloomed into flower, reached the zenith of growth in their life, swiftly then send I my veil of darkness, shrouding and changing to new forms of life.

Steadily upward throughout the ages, growing, expanding into yet greater flame, lighting the darkness with yet greater power, quenched yet unquenched by the veil of the night. So grows the soul of man ever upward, quenched yet unquenched by the darkness of night.

I, Death, come, and yet I remain not, for life eternal exists in the All; only an obstacle, I in the pathway, quick to be conquered by the infinite light. Awaken, 0 flame that burns ever inward, flame forth and conquer the veil of the night."

Then in the midst of the flames in the darkness grew there one that drove forth the night, flaming, expanding, ever brighter, until at last was nothing but Light.

Then spoke my guide, the voice of the master: "See your own soul as it grows in the light, free now forever from the Lord of the night."

The Emerald Tablets

Forward he led me through many great spaces filled with the mysteries of the Children of Light; mysteries that man may never yet know of until he, too, is a Sun of the Light. Backward then HE led me into the Light of the Hall of the Light. Knelt I then before the great Masters, Lords of ALL from the cycles above.

Spoke HE then with words of great power saying: "Thou has been made free of the Halls of Amenti. Choose thou thy work among the children of men."

Then spoke I "0, great master, let me be a teacher of men, leading them onward and upward until they too, are lights among men; freed from the veil of the night that surrounds them, flaming with light that shall shine among men."

Spoke to me then the voice: "Go, as ye will. So be it decreed. Master are ye of your destiny, free to take or reject at will. Take ye the power, take ye the wisdom. Shine as a light among the children of men."

Upward then, led me the Dweller. Dwelt I again among children of men, teaching and showing some of my wisdom; Sun of the Light, a fire among men.

Now again I tread the path downward, seeking the light in the darkness of night.

Hold ye and keep ye, preserve my record, guide shall it be to the children of men.

EMERALD TABLET III
The Key of Wisdom

I, Thoth, the Atlantean, give of my wisdom, give of my knowledge, give of my power. Freely I give to the children of men. Give that they, too, might have wisdom to shine through the world from the veil of the night. Wisdom is power and power is wisdom, one with each other, perfecting the whole.

Be thou not proud, O man, in thy wisdom. Discourse with the ignorant as well as the wise. If one comes to thee full of knowledge, listen and heed, for wisdom is all.

Keep thou not silent when evil is spoken for Truth like the sunlight shines above all.

He who over-steppeth the Law shall be punished, for only through Law comes the freedom of men.

Follow thine heart during thy lifetime. Do thou more than is commanded of thee. When thou has gained riches, follow thou thine heart, for all these are of no avail if thine heart be weary. Diminish thou not the time of following thine heart. It is abhorred of the soul.

They that are guided go not astray, but they that are lost cannot find a straight path.

If thou go among men, make for thyself, Love, the beginning and end of the heart.

If one cometh unto thee for council, let him speak freely, that the thing for which he hath come to thee may be done. If he hesitates to open his heart to thee, it is because thou, the judge, doeth the wrong.

Repeat thou not extravagant speech, neither listen thou to it, for it is the utterance of one not in equilibrium. Speak thou not of it, so that he before thee may know wisdom.

Silence is of great profit. An abundance of speech profiteth nothing.

Exalt not thine heart above the children of men, lest it be brought lower than the dust.

If thou be great among men, be honored for knowledge and gentleness.

If thou seeketh to know the nature of a friend, ask not his companion, but pass a time alone with him. Debate with him, testing his heart by his words and his bearing.

That which goeth into the store-house must come forth, and the things that are thine must be shared with a friend.

Knowledge is regarded by the fool as ignorance, and the things that are profitable are to him hurtful. He liveth in death. It is therefore his food.

The wise man lets his heart overflow but keeps silent his mouth.

0 man, list to the voice of wisdom; list to the voice of light. Mysteries there are in the Cosmos that unveiled fill the world with their light.

Let he who would be free from the bonds of darkness first divine the material from the immaterial, the fire from the earth; for know ye that as earth descends to earth, so also fire ascends unto fire and

The Key of Wisdom

becomes one with fire. He who knows the fire that is within himself shall ascend unto the eternal fire and dwell in it eternally.

Fire, the inner fire, is the most potent of all force, for it overcometh all things and penetrates to all things of the Earth.

Man supports himself only on that which resists. So Earth must resist man else he existeth not.

All eyes do not see with the same vision, for to one an object appears of one form and color and to a different eye of another. So also the infinite fire, changing from color to color, is never the same from day to day.

Thus, speak I, Thoth, of my wisdom, for man is a fire burning bright through the night; never is quenched in the veil of the darkness, never is quenched by the veil of the night.

Hark ye, 0 man, and list to this wisdom: where do name and form cease? Only in consciousness, invisible, an infinite force of radiance bright. The forms that ye create by brightening thy vision are truly effects that follow thy cause.

Man is a star bound to a body, until in the end, he is freed through his strife. Only struggle and toiling thy utmost shall the star within thee bloom out in new life. He who knows the commencement of all things, free is his star from the realms of night.

Remember, 0 man, that all which exists is only another form of that which exists not. Everything that has being is passing into yet other being and thou thyself are not an exception.

Consider the Law, for all is Law. Seek not that which is not of the Law, for such exists only in the illusions of the senses.

The Emerald Tablets

Wisdom cometh to all her children even as they cometh unto wisdom.

All through the ages, the light has been hidden. Awake, O man, and be wise.

Deep in the mysteries of life have I traveled, seeking and searching for that which is hidden. List ye, O man, and be wise.

Far 'neath the earth crust, in the Halls of Amenti, mysteries I saw that are hidden from men.

Oft have I journeyed the deep hidden passage, looked on the Light that is Life among men. There 'neath the Flowers of Life ever living, searched I the hearts and the secrets of men. Found I that man is but living in darkness, light of the great fire is hidden within.

Before the Lords of hidden Amenti learned I the wisdom I give unto men. Masters are they of the great Secret Wisdom, brought from the future of infinity's end. Seven are they, the Lords of Amenti, overlords they of the Children of Morning, Suns of the Cycles, Masters of Wisdom. Formed are not they as the children of men? Three, Four, Five and Six, Seven, Eight, Nine are the titles of the Masters of men.

Far from the future, formless yet forming, came they as teachers for the children of men. Live they forever, yet not of the living, bound not to life and yet free from death. Rule they forever with infinite wisdom, bound yet not bound to the dark Halls of Death. Life they have in them, yet life that is not life, free from all are the Lords of the ALL.

The Key of Wisdom

Forth from them came forth the Logos, instruments they of the power o'er all. Vast is their countenance, yet hidden in smallness, formed by a forming, known yet unknown.

Three holds the key of all hidden magic, creator he of the Halls of the Dead; sending forth power, shrouding with darkness, binding the souls of the children of men; sending the darkness, binding the soul force; director of negative to the children of men.

Four is he who looses the power. Lord, he, of Life to the children of men. Light is his body, flame is his countenance; freer of souls to the children of men.

Five is the master, the Lord of all magic — Key to The Word that resounds among men.

Six is the Lord of Light, the hidden pathway, part of the souls of the children of men.

Seven is he who is Lord of the vastness, master of Space and the key of the Times.

Eight is he who orders the progress; weighs and balances the journey of men.

Nine is the father, vast he of countenance, forming and changing from out of the formless.

Meditate on the symbols I give thee. Keys are they, though hidden from men.

Reach ever upward, 0 Soul of the morning. Turn thy thoughts upward to Light and to Life. Find in the keys of the numbers I bring thee, light on the pathway from life unto life.

The Emerald Tablets

Seek ye with wisdom. Turn thy thoughts inward. Close not thy mind to the Flower of Light.

Place in thy body a thought-formed picture. Think of the numbers that lead thee to Life.

Clear is the pathway to he who has wisdom. Open the door to the Kingdom of Light. Pour forth thy flame as a Sun of the morning. Shut out the darkness and live in the day.

Take thee, 0 man! As part of thy being, the Seven who are but are not as they seem. Opened, O man! Have I my wisdom. Follow the path in the way I have led.

Masters of Wisdom, Sun of the Morning Light and Life to the children of men.

EMERALD TABLET IV
The Space Born

List ye, 0 man, to the voice of wisdom, list to the voice of Thoth, the Atlantean. Freely I give to thee of my wisdom gathered from the time and space of this cycle; master of mysteries, Sun of the morning, Thoth the teacher of men, is of ALL.

Long time ago, I in my childhood, lay 'neath the stars on long-buried Atlantis, dreaming of mysteries far above men. Then in my heart grew there a great longing to conquer the pathway that led to the stars. Year after year, I sought after wisdom, seeking new knowledge, following the way, until at last my Soul, in great travail, broke from its bondage and bounded away. Free was I from the bondage of earth-men. Free from the body, I flashed through the night. Unlocked at last for me was the star-space. Free was I from the bondage of night. Now to the end of space sought I wisdom, far beyond knowledge of finite man.

Far into space, my Soul travelled freely into infinity's circle of light. Strange, beyond knowledge, were some of the planets, great and gigantic, beyond dreams of men. Yet found I Law, in all of its beauty, working through and among them as here among men. Flashed forth my soul through infinity's beauty, far through space I flew with my thoughts.

Rested I there on a planet of beauty. Strains of harmony filled all the air. Shapes there were, moving in Order, great and majestic as stars in the night; mounting in harmony, ordered equilibrium, symbols of the Cosmic, like unto Law.

Many the stars I passed in my journey, many the races of men on their worlds; some reaching high as stars of the morning, some falling low in the blackness of night. Each and all of them struggling upward, gaining the heights and plumbing the depths, moving at times in realms of brightness, living through darkness, gaining the Light.

Know, 0 man, that Light is thine heritage. Know that darkness is only a veil. Sealed in thine heart is brightness eternal, waiting the moment of freedom to conquer, waiting to rend the veil of the night.

Some I found who had conquered the ether. Free of space were they while yet they were men. Using the force that is the foundation of ALL things, far in space constructed they a planet, drawn by the force that flows through the ALL; condensing, coalescing the ether into forms that grew as they willed. Outstripping in science, they, all of the races, mighty in wisdom, sons of the stars.

Long time I paused, watching their wisdom. Saw them create from out of the ether cities gigantic of rose and gold. Formed forth from the primal element, base of all matter, the ether far flung.

Far in the past, they had conquered the ether, freed themselves from the bondage of toil; formed in their mind only a picture and swiftly created, it grew.

Forth then, my soul sped, throughout the Cosmos, seeing ever, new things and old; learning that man is truly space- born, a Sun of the Sun, a child of the stars.

Know ye, O man, whatever form ye inhabit, surely it is one with the stars. Thy bodies are nothing but planets revolving around their central suns. When ye have gained the light of all wisdom, free shall ye be to shine in the ether — one of the Suns that light

The Space Born

outer darkness— one of the space-born grown into Light. Just as the stars in time lose their brilliance, light passing from them into the great source, so, O man, thy soul passes onward, leaving behind the darkness of night.

Formed forth ye, from the primal ether, filled with the brilliance that flows from the source, bound by the ether coalesced around, yet ever it flames until at last it is free. Lift up your flame from out of the darkness, fly from they night and ye shall be free.

Travelled I through the space-time, knowing my soul at last was set free, knowing that now might I pursue wisdom. Until at last, I passed to a plane, hidden from knowledge, known not to wisdom, extension beyond all that we know.

Now, O man, when I had this knowing, happy my soul grew, for now I was free. Listen, ye space- born, list to my wisdom: know ye not that ye, too, will be free.

List ye again, 0 man, to my wisdom, that hearing, ye too, might live and be free. Not of the earth are ye— earthy, but child of the I nfinite Cosmic Light.

Now, to ye, I give knowledge, freedom to walk in the path I have trod, showing ye truly how by my striving, I trod the path that leads to the stars.

Hark ye, 0 man, and know of thy bondage, know how to free thyself from the toils. Out of the darkness shall ye rise upward, one with the Light and one with the stars. Follow ye ever the path of wisdom. Only by this can ye rise from below. Ever man's destiny leads him onward into the Curves of Infinity's ALL.

The Emerald Tablets

Know ye, 0 man, that all space is ordered. Only by Order are ye One with the ALL. Order and balance are the Law of the Cosmos. Follow and ye shall be One with the ALL.

He who would follow the pathway of wisdom, open must be to the Flower of Life, extending his consciousness out of the darkness, flowing through time and space in the ALL.

Deep in the silence, first ye must linger until at last ye are free from desire, free from the longing to speak in the silence. Conquer by silence, the bondage of words. Abstaining from eating until ye have conquered desire for food, that is bondage of soul.

Then lie ye down in the darkness. Close ye your eyes from the rays of the Light. Center thy soul-force in the place of thine consciousness, shaking it free from the bonds of the night. Place in thy mind-place the image thou desireth. Picture the place thou desireth to see. Vibrate back and forth with thy power. Loosen the soul from out of its night. Fiercely must thou shake with all of thy power until at last thy soul shall be free.

Mighty beyond words is the flame of the Cosmic, hanging in planes, unknown to man; mighty and balanced, moving in Order, music of harmonies, far beyond man.

Speaking with music, singing with color, flame from the beginning of Eternity's ALL. Spark of the flame art thou, 0 my children, burning with color and living with music. List to the voice and thou shalt be free.

Consciousness free is fused with the Cosmic, One with the Order and Law of the ALL. Knew ye not man, that out of the darkness, Light shall flame forth, a symbol of ALL.

The Space Born

Pray ye this prayer for attaining of wisdom. Pray for the coming of Light to the ALL.

"Mighty Spirit of Light that shines through the Cosmos, draw my flame closer in harmony to thee. Lift up my fire from out of the darkness, magnet of fire that is One with the ALL. Lift up my soul, thou mighty and potent. Child of the Light, turn not away. Draw me in power to melt in thy furnace; One with all things and all things in One, fire of the life strain and One with the Brain."

When ye have freed thy soul from its bondage, know that for ye the darkness is gone. Ever through space ye may seek wisdom, bound not by fetters forged in flesh.

Onward and upward into the morning, free flash, 0 Soul, to the realms of Light. Move thou in Order, move thou in Harmony, freely shalt move with the Children of Light.

Seek ye and know ye, my Key of Wisdom. Thus, 0 man, ye shall surely be free.

EMERALD TABLET V
The Dweller of Unal

Oft dream I of buried Atlantis, lost in the ages that have passed into night. Aeon on aeon thou existed in beauty, a shining through the darkness of night.

Mighty in power, ruling the earth-born, Lord of the Earth in Atlantis' day. King of the nations, master of wisdom, Light through Suntal, Keeper of the Way, dwelt in his Temple, the Master of Unal, Light of the Earth in Atlantis' day.

Master, He, from a cycle beyond us, living in bodies as one among men. Not as the earth-born, He from beyond us, Sun of a cycle, advanced beyond men.

Know ye, 0 man, that Horlet the Master, was never one with the children of men. Far in the past time when Atlantis first grew as a power, appeared there one with the Key of Wisdom, showing the way of Light to all.

Showed he to all men the path of attainment, way of the Light that flows among men. Mastering darkness, leading the Man-Soul, upward to heights that were One with the Light.

Divided the Kingdoms, He into sections. Ten were they, ruled by children of men. Upon another, built He a Temple, built but not by the children of men.

Out of the Ether called He its substance, moulded and formed by the power of Ytolan into the forms He built with His mind. Mile upon mile it covered the island, space upon space it grew in its might. Black, yet not black, but dark like the space-time, deep in

The Dweller of Unal

its heart the Essence of Light. Swiftly the Temple grew into being, moulded an shaped by the Word of the Dweller, called from the formless into a form.

Builded He then, within it, great chambers, filled them from forms called forth from the Ether, filled them with wisdom called forth by His mind.

Formless was He within his Temple, yet was He formed in the image of man. Dwelling among them yet not of them, strange and far different was He from the children of men.

Chose He then from among the people, Three who became his gateway. Chose He the Three from the Highest to become his links with Atlantis. Messengers they, who carried his councel, to the kings of the children of men. Brought He forth others and taught them wisdom; teachers, they, to the children of men. Placed He them on the island of Undal to stand as teachers of Light to men.

Each of those who were thus chosen, taught must he be for years five and ten. Only thus could he have understanding to being Light to the children of men. Thus there came into being the Temple, a dwelling place for the Master of man.

I, Thoth, have ever sought wisdom, searching in darkness and searching in Light. Long in my youth I traveled the pathway, seeking ever new knowledge to gain. Until after much striving, one of the Three, to me brought the Light. Brought He to me the commands of the Dweller, called me from darkness into the Light. Brought He me, before the Dweller, deep in the Temple before the great Fire.

The Emerald Tablets

There on the great throne, beheld I, the Dweller, clothed with the Light and flashing with fire. Down I knelt before that great wisdom, feeling the Light flowing through me in waves.

Heard I then the voice of the Dweller: "0 darkness, come into the Light. Long have ye sought the pathway to the Light. Each soul on earth that loosens its fetters shall soon be made free from the bondage of night. Forth from the darkness have ye arisen, closer approached the Light of your goal. Here ye shall dwell as one of my children, keeper of records gathered by wisdom, instrument thou of the Light from beyond. Ready be thou made to do what is needed, perserver of wisdom though the ages of darkness that shall come fast on the children of men. Live thee here and drink of all wisdom. Secrets and mysteries unto thee shall unveil."

Then answered I, the Master of Cycles, saying: "O Light, that descended to men, give thou to me of thy wisdom that I might be a teacher of men. Give thou of thy Light that I may be free."

Spoke then to me again, the Master: "Age after age shall ye live through your wisdom. Aye, when o'er Atlantis the ocean waves roll, holding the Light, though hidden in darkness, ready to come when e'er thou shalt call. Go thee now and learn greater wisdom. Grow thou through Light to Infinity's ALL."

Long then dwelt I in the Temple of the Dweller until at last I was One with the Light. Followed I then the path to the star planes, followed I then the pathway to Light. Deep into Earth's heart I followed the pathway, learning the secrets, below as above; learning the pathway to the Halls of Amenti; learning the Law that balances the world.

To earth's hidden chambers pierced I by my wisdom, deep through the Earth's crust, into the pathway, hidden for ages from

The Dweller of Unal

the children of men. Unveiled before me, ever more wisdom until I reached a new knowledge: found that all is part of an ALL, great and yet greater than all that we know. Searched I Infinity's heart through the ages. Deep and yet deeper, more mysteries I found.

Now, as I look back through the ages, know I that wisdom is boundless, ever grown greater throughout the ages, One with Infinity's greater than all.

Light there was in ancient Atlantis. Yes, darkness, too, was hidden in all. Fell from the Light into the darkness, some who had risen to heights among men. Proud they became because of their knowledge, proud were they of their place among men. Deep delved they into the forbidden, opened the gateway that led to below. Sought they to gain ever more knowledge but seeking to bring it up from below. He who descends below must have balance, else he is bound by lack of our Light. Opened, they then, by their knowledge, pathways forbidden to man.

But, in His Temple, all-seeing, the Dweller, lay in his Agwanti, which through Atlantis His soul roamed free. Saw He the Atlanteans, by their magic, opening the gateway that would bring to Earth a great woe. Fast fled His soul then, back to His body. Up He arose from His Agwanti. Called He the Three mighty messengers. Gave the commands that shattered the world.

Deep 'neath Earth's crust to the Halls of Amenti, swiftly descended the Dweller. Called He then on the powers of the Seven Lords wielded; changed the Earth's balance.

Down sank Atlantis beneath the dark waves. Shattered the gateway that had been opened; shattered the doorway that led down below. All of the islands were shattered except Unal, and part of the island of the sons of the Dweller.

The Emerald Tablets

Preserved He them to be the teachers, Lights on the path for those to come after, Lights for the lesser children of man.

Called He then, I Thoth, before him, gave me commands for all I should do, saying: "Take thou, O Thoth, all of your wisdom. Take all your records. Take all your magic. Go thou forth preserving the records until in time Light grows among men. Light shalt thou be all through the ages, hidden yet found by enlightened men. Over all Earth, give WE ye power, free thou to give or take it away. Gather thou now the sons of Atlantis. Take them and flee to the people of the rock caves. Fly to the land of the Children of Khem."

Then gathered I the sons of Atlantis. Into the spaceship I brought all my records, brought the records of sunken Atlantis. Gathered I all of my powers, instruments many of mighty magic.

Up then we rose on wings of the morning. High we arose above the Temple, leaving behind the three and Dweller, deep in the Halls 'neath the Temple. Down 'neath the waves sank the great Temple, closing the pathway to the Lords of the Cycles. Yet ever to him who has knowing, open shall be the path to Amenti.

Fast fled we then on the wings of the morning, fled to the land of the children of Khem. There by my power, I conquered and ruled them. Raised I to Light, the children of Khem.

Deep 'neath the rocks, I buried my spaceship, waiting the time when man might be free. Over the spaceship, erected a marker in the form of a lion yet like unto man. There 'neath the image rests yet my spaceship, forth to be brought when need shall arise.

Know ye, O man, that far in the future invaders shall come from out of the deep.

The Dweller of Unal

Then awake, ye who have wisdom. Bring forth my ship and conquer with ease.

Deep 'neath the image lies my secret. Search and find in the pyramid I built. Each to the other is the Keystone; each the gateway that leads into Life. Follow the Key I leave behind me. Seek and the doorway to Life shall be thine. Seek thou in my pyramid, deep in the passage that ends in a wall. Use thou the Key of the Seven, and open to thee the pathway will fall.

Now unto thee I have given my wisdom. Now unto thee I have given my way. Follow the pathway. Solve thou my secrets. Unto thee I have shown the way.

EMERALD TABLET VI
The Key of Magic

Hark ye, 0 man, to the wisdom of magic. Hark to the knowledge of powers forgotten.

Long, long ago in the days of the first man, warfare began between darkness and light. Men, then as now, were filled with both darkness and light; and while in some darkness held sway, in others light filled the soul.

Aye, age old is this warfare, the eternal struggle between darkness and light. Fiercely is it fought all through the ages, using strange powers hidden to man.

Adepts have there been filled with the blackness, struggling always against the light; but others there are who, filled with brightness, have ever conquered the darkness of night. Where e'er ye may be in all ages and planes, surely ye shall know of the battle with night.

Long ages ago, the Suns of the Morning, descending, found the world filled with night. There in that past time began the struggle, the age old battle of darkness and Light.

Many in that time were so filled with darkness that only feebly flamed the light from the night.

Some there were, masters of darkness, who sought to fill all with their darkness; sought to draw others into their night. Fiercely withstood they, the masters of brightness; fiercely fought they from the darkness of night. Sought they ever to tighten the fetters, the chains that bind man to the darkness of night. Used they always the dark magic, brought into man by the power of darkness; magic that enshrouded man's soul with darkness.

Banded together in as order, Brothers of Darkness, they through the ages, antagonists they to the children of men. Walked they always secret and hidden, found yet not found by the children of men. Forever they walked and worked in darkness, hiding from the light in the darkness of night. Silently, secretly, use they their power, enslaving and binding the souls of men.

Unseen they come and unseen they go. Man in his ignorance calls Them from below.

Dark is the way the Dark Brothers travel, dark with a darkness not of the night, traveling o'er Earth they walk through man's dreams. Power have they gained from the darkness around them to call other dwellers from out of their plane in ways that are dark and unseen by man. Into man's mind-space reach the Dark Brothers. Around it, they close the veil of their night. There through its lifetime that soul dwells in bondage, bound by the fetters of the Veil of the night. Mighty are they in the forbidden knowledge, forbidden because it is one with the night.

Hark ye, 0 man, and list to my warning: be ye free from the bondage of night. Surrender not your soul to the Brothers of Darkness. Keep thy face ever turned toward the Light. Know ye not, 0 man, that your sorrow only has come through the Veil of the night? Aye, man, heed ye my warning: strive ever upward, turn your soul toward the Light. For well know they that those who have traveled far towards the Sun on their pathway of Light have great and yet greater power to bind with darkness the children of Light.

The Emerald Tablets

List ye, 0 man, to he who comes to you. But weigh in the balance if his words be of Light. For many there are who walk in Dark Brightness and yet are not the children of Light. Easy it is to follow their pathway, easy to follow the path that they lead. But yes, O man, heed ye my warning: Light comes only to him who strives. Hard is the pathway that leads to the Wisdom, hard is the pathway that leads to the Light. Many shall ye find, the stones in your pathway; many the mountains to climb toward the Light.

Yet know ye, 0 man, to him that o'ercometh, free will he be of the pathway of Light. Follow ye not the Dark Brothers ever. Always be ye a child of the Light. For know ye, 0 man, in the end Light must conquer and darkness and night be banished from Light.

Listen, 0 man, and heed ye this wisdom; even as darkness, so is the Light.

When darkness is banished and all Veils are rendered, out there shall flash from the darkness, the Light.

Even as exist among men the Dark Brothers, so there exists the Brothers of Light. Antagonists they of the Brothers of Darkness, seeking to free men from the night. Powers have they, mighty and potent. Knowing the Law, the planets obey. Work they ever in harmony and order, freeing the man-soul from its bondage of night. Secret and hidden, walk they also. Known not are they to the children of men. Yet know that ever they walk with thee, showing the Way to the children of men. Ever have They fought the Dark Brothers, conquered and conquering time without end.

Yet always Light shall in the end be master, driving away the darkness of night.

The Key of Magic

Aye, man, know ye this knowing: always beside thee walk the Children of Light. Masters they of the Sun power, ever unseen yet the guardians of men. Open to all is their pathway, open to he who will walk in the Light. Free are They of Dark Amenti, free of the Halls where Life regins supreme. Suns are they and Lords of the morning, Children of Light to shine among men. Like man are they and yet are unlike. Never divided were they in the past. One have they been in Oneness eternal, throughout all space since the beginning of time.

Up did they come in Oneness with the All One, up from the first-space, formed and unformed. Given to man have they secrets that shall guard and protect him from all harm.

He who would travel the path of a master, free must he be from the bondage of night. Conquer must he the formless and shapeless; conquer must he the phantom of fear. Knowing, must he gain of all the secrets, travel the pathway that leads through the darkness, yet ever before him keep the light of his goal. Obstacles great shall he meet in the pathway, yet press on to the Light of the Sun.

Hear ye, O man, the Sun is the symbol of the Light that shines at the end of thy road.

Now to thee give I the secrets: how to meet the dark power, meet and conquer the fear from the night. Only by knowing can ye conquer; only by knowing can ye have Light.

Now I give unto thee the knowledge, known to the Masters; the knowing that conquers all the dark fears. Use this, the wisdom I give thee. Master thou shalt be of the Brothers of Night.

The Emerald Tablets

When unto thee there comes a feeling, drawing thee nearer to the dark gate, examine thine heart and find if the feeling thou hast has come from within.

If thou shalt find the darkness thine own thoughts, banish them forth from place in thy mind. Send through thy body a wave of vibration, irregular first and regular second, repeating time after time until free. Start the Wave Force in thy Brain Center. Direct it in waves from thine head to thy foot.

But if thou findest thine heart is not darkened, be sure that a force is directed to thee. Only by knowing can thou overcome it. Only by wisdom can thou hope to be free.

Knowledge brings wisdom and wisdom is power. Attain and ye shall have power o'er all.

Seek ye first a place bound with darkness. Place ye a circle around about thee. Stand erect in the midst of the circle. Use thou this formula, and thou shalt be free. Raise thou thine hands to the dark space above thee. Close thou thine eyes and draw in the Light.

Call to the Spirit of Light through the Space- Time, using these words and thou shalt be free: "Fill thou my body with Spirit of Light. Come from the Flower that shines through the darkness. Come from the Halls where the Seven Lords rule. Name them by name, I, the Seven: Three, Four, Five and Six, Seven, Eight— Nine. By their names I call them to aid me, free me and save me from the darkness of night: Untanas, Quertas, Chietal, and Goyana, Huertal, Semveta— Ardal. By their names I implore thee, free me from darkness and fill me with Light."

Know ye, O man, that when ye have done this, ye shall be free from the fetters that bind ye, cast off the bondage of the Brothers of

The Key of Magic

Night. See ye not that the names have the power to free by vibration the fetters that bind? Use them at need to free thou thine brother so the he, too, may come forth from the night. Thou, O man, art thy brother's helper. Let him not lie in the bondage of night.

Now unto thee, give I my magic. Take it and dwell on the pathway of Light. Light unto thee, Life unto thee, Sun may thou be on the cycle above.

EMERALD TABLET VII
The Seven Lords

Hark ye, 0 man, and list to my Voice. Open thy mind-space and drink of my wisdom.

Dark is the pathway of Life that ye travel. Many the pitfalls that lie in thy way. Seek ye ever to gain greater wisdom. Attain and it shall be light on thy way.

Open thy Soul, O man, to the Cosmic and let it flow in as one with thy Soul. Light is eternal and darkness is fleeting. Seek ye ever, 0 man, for the Light. Know ye that ever as Light fills thy being, darkness for thee shall soon disappear.

Open thy soul to the Brothers of Brightness. Let them enter and fill thee with Light. Lift up thine eyes to the Light of the Cosmos. Keep thou ever thy face to the goal.

Only by gaining the light of all wisdom, art thou one with the Infinite goal. Seek ye ever the Oneness eternal. Seek ye ever the Light of the goal.

Light is infinite and Light is finite, separate only by darkness in man. Seek ye to rend the Veil of the Darkness. Bring thou together the Light into One.

Hear ye, O man, list to my Voice singing the song of Light and of Life. Throughout all space, Light is prevalent, encompassing ALL with its banners of flame. Seek ye forever in the Veil of the Darkness, somewhere ye shall surely find Light.

The Seven Lords

Hidden and buried, lost to man's knowledge, deep in the finite the Infinite exists. Lost, but existing, flowing through all things, living in ALL is the Infinite Brain. In all space, there is only One wisdom.

Though seeming divided, it is One in the One. All that exists comes forth from the Light, and the Light comes forth from the ALL.

Everything created is based upon Order: Law rules the space where the Infinite dwells. Forth from equilibrium came the great cycles, moving in harmony toward Infinity's end.

Know ye, 0 man, that far in the space-time, Infinity itself shall pass into change. Here ye and list to the Voice of Wisdom: Know that ALL is of ALL evermore. Know that through time thou may pursue wisdom and find ever more light on the way. Aye, thou shalt find that ever receding, thy goal shall elude thee from day unto day.

Long time ago, in the Halls of Amenti, I, Thoth, stood before the Lords of the cycles.

Mighty, They in their aspects of power; mighty, They in the wisdom unveiled. Led by the Dweller, first did I see them. But afterwards free was I of their presence, free to enter their conclave at will. Oft did I journey down the dark pathway unto the Hall where the Light ever glows.

Learned I of the Masters of cycles, wisdom brought from the cycles above us, knowledge brought from Infinity's All. Many the questions I asked of the Lords of the cycles.

Great was the wisdom they gave unto me. Now unto thee I give of this wisdom, drawn from the flame of Infinity's fire.

The Emerald Tablets

Deep in the Dark Halls sit the Seven, units of consciousness from cycles above. Manifest They in this cycle as guide of man to the knowledge of All. Seven are they, mighty in power, speaking these words through me to men. Time after time, stood I before them listening to words that came not with sound.

Once said They unto me: "0 man, wouldst thou gain wisdom? Seek for it in the heart of the flame. Wouldst thou gain knowledge of power? Seek ye it in the heart of the flame. Wouldst be one with the heart of the flame? Seek then within thine own hidden flame."

Many the times spoke They to me, teaching me wisdom not of the world; showing me ever new paths to brightness; teaching me wisdom brought from above. Giving knowledge of operation, learning of Law, the order of ALL.

Spoke to me again, the Seven, saying: "From far beyond time are We come, 0 man. Traveled We from beyond the Space-Time, aye, from the place of Infinity's end. When ye and all of thy brethren were formless, formed forth were We from the order of ALL. Not as men are We though once We, too, were as men. Out of the Great Void were We formed forth in order and by Law. For know ye that that which is formed truly is formless, having form only to thine eyes."

And again, unto me spoke the Seven, saying: "Child of the Light, 0 Thoth, art thou, free to travel the bright path upward until at the last All Ones become One. Forth were We formed after our order: Three, Four, Five and Six, Seven, Eight— Nine. Know ye that these are the number of cycles that We descend from unto man. Each having here a duty to fulfill; each having here a force to control. Yet are We, One, with the Soul of our cycle. Yet are We, too, seeking a goal. Far beyond man's conception, Infinity extends into

The Seven Lords

a greater than All. There, in a time that is yet not a time, we shall ALL become ONE with a greater than ALL. Time and space are moving in circles. Know ye their law, and ye, too, shall be free. Aye, free shall ye be to move through the cycles— pass the guardians that dwell at the door."

Then to me spoke He of Nine, saying: "Aeons and aeons have I existed, knowing not Life, and tasting not death. For know ye, O man, that far in the future, life and death shall be one with the All. Each so perfected by balancing the other that neither exists in the Oneness of All. In men of this cycle, the life force is rampant, but life in its growth becomes one with the All. Here, I manifest in this your cycle, but yet am I there in your future of time. Yet to me, time exists not, for in my world time exists not, for formless are We. Life have We not but yet have existence, fuller and greater and freer than thee. Man is a flame bound to a mountain, but We in our cycle shall ever be free. Know ye, O man, that when ye have progressed into the cycles that lengthen above, life itself will pass to the darkness and only the essence of Soul shall remain."

Then to me spoke the Lord of the Eight saying: "All that ye know is but part of little. Not as yet have ye touched on the Great. Far out in space where Light reigns supreme, came I into the Light. Formed was I also but not as ye are. Body of Light was my formless form formed. Know I not Life and know I not Death, yet master am I of all that exists. Seek ye to find the path through the barriers. Travel the road that leads to the Light."

Spoke again to me the Nine saying: "Seek ye to find the path to beyond. Not impossible is it to grow to a consciousness above. For when Two have become One and One has become the All, know ye the barrier has lifted, and ye are made free of the road. Grow thou from form to the formless. Free may thou be of the road."

The Emerald Tablets

Thus, through ages I listened, learning the way to the All. Now lift I my thought to the All-Thing. List ye and hear when it calls. "0 Light, all pervading, One with All and All with One, flow thou to me through the channel. Enter thou so that I may be free. Make me One with the All-Soul, shining from the blackness of night. Free let me be of all space-time, free from the Veil of the night. I, a child of the Light, command: Free from the darkness to be."

Formless am I to the Light-Soul, formless yet shining with Light. Know I the bonds of the darkness must shatter and fall before light.

Now give I this wisdom. Free may ye be, O man, living in light and in brightness.

Turn not thy face from the Light. Thy soul dwells in realms of brightness. Ye are a child of the Light.

Turn thy thoughts inward not outward. Find thou the Light-Soul within. Know that thou are the Master. All else is brought from within. Grow thou to realms of brightness.

Hold thou thy thought on the Light. Know thou are one with the Cosmos, a flame and a Child of the Light.

Now to thee give I warning: Let not thy thought turn away. Know that the brightness flows through thy body for aye. Turn not to the Dark- Brightness that comes from the Brothers of Black. But keep thine eyes ever lifted, thy soul in tune with the Light.

Take ye this wisdom and heed it. List to my Voice and obey. Follow the pathway to brightness, and thou shalt be One with the way.

EMERALD TABLET VIII
The Key of Mysteries

Unto thee, 0 man, have I given my knowledge. Unto thee have I given of Light. Hear ye now and receive my wisdom brought from space planes above and beyond.

Not as man am I for free have I become of dimensions and planes. In each, take I on a new body. In each, I change in my form. Know I now that the formless is all there is of form.

Great is the wisdom of the Seven. Mighty are they from beyond. Manifest They through their power, filled by force from beyond.

Here ye these words of wisdom. Hear ye and make them thine own. Find in them the formless. Find ye the key to beyond. Mystery is but hidden knowledge. Know and ye shall unveil. Find the deep buried wisdom and be master of darkness and Light.

Deep are the mysteries around thee, hidden the secrets of Old. Search through the Keys of my Wisdom. Surely shall ye find the way. The gateway to power is secret, but he who attains shall receive. Look to the Light! O my brother. Open and ye shall receive.

Press on through the valley of darkness. Overcome the dweller of the night. Keep ever thine eyes to the Light-Plane, and thou shalt be One with the Light.

Man is in process of changing to forms that are not of this world. Grows he in time to the formless, a plane on the cycle above. Know ye, ye must become formless before ye are one with the Light.

The Emerald Tablets

List ye, 0 man, to my voice, telling of the pathways to Light, showing the way of attainment when ye shall be One with the Light. Search ye the mysteries of Earth's heart. Learn of the Law that exists, holding the stars in their balance by the force of the primordial mist. Seek ye the flame of the Earth's Life. Bathe in the glare of its flame. Follow the three-cornered pathway until thou, too, art a flame.

Speak thou in words without voice to those who dwell down below. Enter the blue-litten Temple and bathe in the fire of all life.

Know, 0 man, thou art complex, a being of earth and of fire. Let thy flame shine out brightly. Be thou only the fire.

Wisdom is hidden in darkness. When lit by the flame of the Soul, find thou the wisdom and be Light-Born, a Sun of the Light without form. Seek thee ever more wisdom. Find it in the heart of the flame. Know that only by striving can Light pour into thy brain.

Now have I spoken with wisdom. List to my Voice and obey. Tear open the Veils of the darkness. Shine a Light on the Way.

Speak I of Ancient Atlantis, speak of the days of the Kingdom of Shadows, speak of the coming of the children of shadows. Out of the great deep were they called by the wisdom of earth-men, called for the purpose of gaining great power.

Far in the past before Atlantis existed, men there were who delved into darkness, using dark magic, calling up beings from the great deep below us. Forth came they into this cycle. Formless were they of another vibration, existing unseen by the children of earth-men. Only through blood could they have formed being. Only through man could they live in the world.

The Key of Mysteries

In ages past were they conquered by the Masters, driven below to the place whence they came. But some there were who remained, hidden in spaces and planes unknown to man. Lived they in Atlantis as shadows, but at times they appeared among men. Aye, when the blood was offered, forth came they to dwell among men.

In the form of man moved they amongst us, but only to sight where they as are men. Serpent- headed when the glamour was lifted but appearing to man as men among men. Crept they into the Councils, taking forms that were like unto men. Slaying by their arts the chiefs of the kingdoms, taking their form and ruling o'er man. Only by magic could they be discovered. Only by sound could their faces be seen. Sought they from the kingdom of shadows to destroy man and rule in his place.

But, know ye, the Masters were mighty in magic, able to lift the Veil from the face of the serpent, able to send him back to his place. Came they to man and taught him the secret, the Word that only a man can pronounce. Swift then they lifted the Veil from the serpent and cast him forth from place among men.

Yet, beware, the serpent still liveth in a place that is open at times to the world. Unseen they walk among thee in places where the rites have been said. Again as time passes onward shall they take the semblance of men.

Called may they be by the master who knows the white or the black, but only the white master may control and bind them while in the flesh.

Seek not the kingdom of shadows, for evil will surely appear. For only the master of brightness shall conquer the shadow of fear.

The Emerald Tablets

Know ye, O my brother, that fear is an obstacle great. Be master of all in the brightness, the shadow will soon disappear. Hear ye and heed my wisdom, the voice of Light is clear. Seek not the valley of shadow, and Light only will appear.

List ye, O man, to the depth of my wisdom. Speak I of knowledge hidden from man.

Far have I been on my journey though Space-Time, even to the end of the space of this cycle. Found I there the great barrier, holding man from leaving this cycle. Aye, glimpsed the Hounds of the Barrier, laying in wait for he who would pass them. In that space where time exists not, faintly I sensed the guardians of cycles. Move they only through angles. Free are they not of the curved dimensions.

Strange and terrible are the Hounds of the Barrier. Follow they consciousness to the limits of space. Think not to escape by entering your body, for follow they fast the Soul through angles. Only the circle will give ye protection, safe from the claws of the Dweller in Angles.

Once, in a time past, I approached the great Barrier, and saw on the shores where time exists not, the formless forms of the Hounds of the Barrier. Aye, hiding in the mist beyond time I found them; and They, scenting me afar off, raised themselves and gave the great bell cry that can be heard from cycle to cycle and moved through space toward my Soul.

Fled I then fast before them, back from time's unthinkable end. But ever after me pursued they, moving in strange angles not known to man. Aye, on the gray shore of Time-Space's end found I the Hounds of the Barrier, ravening for the Soul who attempts the beyond.

The Key of Mysteries

Fled I through circles back to my body. Fled, and fast after me they followed. Aye, after me the devourers followed, seeking through angles to devour my Soul.

Aye, know ye man, that the Soul who dares the Barrier may be held in bondage by the Hounds from beyond time, held till this cycle is all completed and left behind when the consciousness leaves.

Entered I my body. Created the circles that know not angles, created the form that from my form was formed. Made my body into a circle and lost the pursuers in the circles of time. But, even yet, when free from my body, cautious ever must I be not to move through angles, else my Soul might never be free.

Know ye, the Hounds of the Barrier move only through angles and never through curves of space. Only by moving through curves can ye escape them, for in angles they will pursue thee. 0 man, heed ye my warning; Seek not to break open the gate to beyond.

Few there are who have succeeded in passing the Barrier to the greater Light that shines beyond. For know ye, ever the dwellers, seek such Souls to hold in their thrall.

Listen, O man, and heed ye my warning; seek ye to move not in angles but curves. And if while free from thy body, thou hearest the sound like the bay of a hound ringing clear and bell-like through thy being, flee back to thy body through circles, penetrate not the mist before.

When thou hast entered the form thou hast dwelt in, use thou the cross and the circle combined. Open thy mouth and use thou thy Voice. Utter the Word and thou shalt be free. Only the one who of Light has the fullest can hope to pass by the guards of the way.

And then must he move through strange curves and angles that are formed in direction not known to man.

List ye, O man, and heed ye my warning: attempt not to pass the guards in the way. Rather should ye seek to gain of thine own Light and make thyself ready to pass on the way.

Light is thine ultimate end, O my brother. Seek and find ever the Light on thy way.

EMERALD TABLET IX
The Key of Freedom of Space

List ye, 0 man, hear ye my voice, teaching of Wisdom and Light in this cycle; teaching ye how to banish the darkness, teaching ye how to bring Light in thy life.

Seek ye, 0 man, to find the great pathway that leads to eternal Life as a Sun. Draw ye away from the veil of the darkness. Seek to become a Light in the world. Make of thyself a vessel for Light, a focus for the Sun of this space.

Lift thou thine eyes to the Cosmos. Lift thou thine eyes to the Light. Speak in the words of the Dweller, the chant that calls down the Light. Sing thou the song of freedom.

Sing thou the song of the Soul. Create the high vibration that will make thee One with the Whole. Blend all thyself with the Cosmos. Grow into One with the Light. Be thou a channel of order, a pathway of Law to the world.

Thy Light, O man, is the great Light, shining through the shadow of flesh. Free must thou rise from the darkness before thou art One with the Light.

Shadows of darkness surround thee. Life fills thee with its flow. But know, 0 man, thou must arise and forth from thy body go far to the planes that surround thee and yet are One with thee, too.

Look all around thee, 0 man. See thine own light reflected. Aye, even in the darkness around thee, thine own Light pours forth through the veil.

The Emerald Tablets

Seek thou for wisdom always. Let not thine body betray. Keep in the path of the Light wave. Shun thou the darkened way. Know thee that wisdom is lasting, existing since the All-Soul began, creating harmony from chaos by the Law that exists in the Way.

List ye, 0 man, to the teaching of wisdom. List to the voice that speaks of the pasttime. Aye, I shall tell thee knowledge forgotten, tell ye of wisdom hidden in past-time, lost in the mist of darkness around me.

Know ye, man, ye are the ultimate of all things. Only the knowledge of this is forgotten, lost when man was cast into bondage, bound and fettered by the chains of the darkness.

Long, long ago, I cast off my body. Wandered I free through the vastness of ether, circled the angles that hold man in bondage. Know ye, O man, ye are only a spirit. The body is nothing. The Soul is All. Let not your body be a fetter. Cast off the darkness and travel in Light. Cast off your body, O man, and be free, truly a Light that is One with the Light.

When ye are free from the fetters of darkness and travel in space as a Sun of the Light, then ye shall know that space is not boundless but truly bounded by angles and curves. Know ye, O man, that all that exists is only an aspect of greater things yet to come. Matter is fluid and flows like a stream, constantly changing from one thing to another.

All through the ages has knowledge existed; never been changed, though buried in darkness; never been lost, though forgotten by man.

The Key of Freedom of Space

Know ye that throughout the space that ye dwell in are others as great as your own, interlaced through the heart of your matter yet separate in space of their own.

Once in a time long forgotten, I, Thoth, opened the doorway, penetrated into other spaces and learned of the secrets concealed. Deep in the essence of matter are many mysteries concealed.

Nine are the interlocked dimensions, and Nine are the cycles of space. Nine are the diffusions of consciousness, and Nine are the worlds within worlds. Aye, Nine are the Lords and the cycles that come from above and below.

Space is filled with concealed ones, for space is divided by time. Seek ye the key to the time-space, and ye shall unlock the gate. Know ye that throughout the time-space consciousness surely exists. Though from our knowledge it is hidden, yet still it forever exists.

The key to worlds within thee are found only within. For man is the gateway of mystery and the key that is One within One.

Seek ye within the circle. Use the Word I shall give. Open the gateway within thee, and sure thou, too, shalt live. Man, ye think that ye liveth, but know it is life within death. For as sure as ye are bound to your body, for you no life exists. Only the Soul is space-free, has life that is really a life. All else is only a bondage, a fetter from which to be free.

Think not that man is earth-born, though come from the earth he may be. Man is a light- born spirit. But, without knowing, he can never be free. Darkness fetters the Soul. Only the one who is seeking may ever hope to be free.

The Emerald Tablets

Shadows around thee are falling. Darkness fills all the spaces. Shine forth, 0 Light of the man-soul. Fill thou the darkness of space. Ye are a Sun of the Great Light. Remember and ye shall be free. Stay not thou in the shadows. Spring forth from the darkness of night. Light, let thy Soul be, 0 Sun-Born, filled with glory of Light, freed from the bonds of darkness, a Soul that is One with the Light.

Thou art the key to all wisdom. Within thee is all time and space. Live not in bondage to darkness. Free thou thy Light-form from night.

"Great Light that fills all the Cosmos, flow thou fully to man. Make of his body a light-torch that shall never be quenched among men."

Long in the past, sought I wisdom, knowledge not known to man. Far to the past I traveled into the space where time began. Sought I ever new knowledge to add to the wisdom I know. Yet only, I found, did the future hold the key to the wisdom I sought.

Down to the Halls of Amenti I journeyed, the greater knowledge to seek. Asked of the Lords of the Cycles, the way to the wisdom I sought. Asked the Lords this question: "Where is the source of ALL?" Answered, in tones that were mighty, the voice of the Lord of the Nine: "Free thou thy Soul from thy body and come forth with me to the Light."

Forth I came from my body, a glittering flame in the night. Stood I before the Lords, bathed in the fire of Life. Seized was I then by a force, great beyond knowledge of man.

Cast was I to the Abyss through spaces unknown to man.

Saw I moulding of Order from the chaos and angles of night. Saw I the Light spring from Order and heard the voice of the Light. Saw

The Key of Freedom of Space

I the flame of the Abyss, casting forth Order and Light. Saw Order spring out of chaos. Saw Light giving forth Life.

Then heard I the voice: "Hear thou and understand. The flame is the source of all things, containing all things in potentiality. The Order that sent forth light is the Word and from the Word comes Life and the existence of all."

And again spoke the voice saying: "The Life in thee is the Word. Find thou the Life within thee, and have powers to use of the Word."

Long I watched the Light-flame, pouring forth from the Essence of Fire, realizing that Life is but Order and that man is one with the fire.

Back I came to my body. Stood again with the Nine, listened to the voice of the Cycles, vibrate with powers they spoke: "Know ye, 0 Thoth, that Life is but the Word of the Fire. The Life force ye seek before thee is but the Word in the World as a fire. Seek ye the path to the Word and powers shall surely be thine."

Then asked I of the Nine: "0 Lord, show me the path. Give me the path to the wisdom. Show me the way to the Word."

Answered, me then, the Lord of the Nine: "Through Order, ye shall find the way. Saw ye not that the Word came from Chaos? Saw ye not that Light came from Fire? Look in thy life for disorder. Balance and order thy life. Quell all the Chaos of emotions and thou shalt have order in Life. Order brought forth from Chaos will bring thee the Word of the Source, will give thee the power of Cycles, and make of thy Soul a force that free will extend through the ages, a perfected Sun from the Source."

The Emerald Tablets

Listened I to the voice and deep sank the words in my heart. For ever have I sought for order that I might draw on the word. Know ye that he who attains it must ever in Order be. For use of the Word through disorder has never and can never be.

Take ye these words, O man. As part of thy life, let them be. Seek thee to conquer disorder, and One with the Word thou shalt be. Put forth thy effort in gaining Light on the pathway of Life. Seek to be One with the Sun-State. Seek to be solely the Light. Hold thou thy thought on the Oneness of Light with the body of man. Know that all is Order from Chaos born into Light.

EMERALD TABLET X
The Key of Time

List ye, 0 man. Take of my wisdom. Learn of the deep hidden mysteries of space.

Learn of the Thought that grew in the abyss, bringing Order and Harmony in space.

Know ye, O man, that all that exists has being only because of the Law. Know ye the Law and ye shall be free, never be bound by the fetters of night. Far, through strange spaces, have I journeyed into the depth of the abyss of time, learning strange and yet stranger mysteries, until in the end all was revealed.

Know ye that mystery is only mystery when it is knowledge unknown to man. When you have plumbed the heart of all mystery, knowledge and wisdom will surely be thine.

Seek ye and learn that Time is the secret whereby ye may be free of this space. Long have I, Thoth, sought wisdom; aye, and shall seek to eternity's end for know I that ever before receding shall move the goal I seek to attain. Even the Lords of the Cycles know that not yet have They reached the goal, for with all of their wisdom, they know that Truth ever grows.

Once, in a past time, I spoke to the Dweller. Asked of the mystery of time and space. Asked him the question that surged in my being, saying: "0 Master, what is time?"

Then to me spoke He, the Master: "Know ye, O Thoth, in the beginning there was void and nothingness: a timeless, spaceless, nothingness. And into the nothingness came a thought, purposeful, all-pervading, and It filled the Void. There existed no matter, only force, a movement, a vortex of vibration of the purposeful thought that filled the Void."

And I questioned the Master, saying: "Was this thought eternal?" And answered me the Dweller, saying: "In the beginning, there was eternal thought, and for thought to be eternal, time must exist. So into the all-pervading thought grew the Law of Time. Aye, time which exists through all space, floating in a smooth, rhythmic movement that is eternally in a state of fixation. Time changes not, but all things change in time. For time is the force that holds events separate, each in its proper place. Time is not in motion, but ye move through time as your consciousness moves from one event to another. Aye, by time ye exist, all in all, an eternal One existence. Know ye that even though in time ye are separate, yet still are One in all times existent." Ceased then the voice of the Dweller, and departed I to ponder on time. For knew I that in these words lay wisdom and a way to explore the mysteries of time.

Oft did I ponder the words of the Dweller. Then sought I to solve the mystery of time. Found I that time moves through strange angles. Yet only by curves could I hope to attain the key that would give me access to the time-space. Found I that only by moving upward and yet again by moving to right-ward could I be free from the time of this movement.

Forth I came from out of my body, moved in the movements that changed me in time. Strange were the sights I saw in my journeys, many the mysteries that opened to view. Aye, saw I man's beginning, learned from the past that nothing is new.

Seek ye, 0 man, to learn the pathway that leads through the spaces that are formed forth in time. Forget not, 0 man, with all of thy seeking that Light is the goal ye shall seek to attain. Search ye ever for Light on thy pathway and ever for thee the goal shall endure. Let not thine heart turn ever to darkness. Light let thine Soul be, a sun on the way. Know ye that in the eternal brightness, ye shall ever find thy Soul hid in the Light, never fettered by bondage to darkness, ever it shines forth a Sun of the Light. Aye, know, though hidden in darkness, your Soul, a spark of the true flame, exists. Be ye One with the greatest of all Lights. Find at the Source, the End of thy goal.

Light is life, for without the great Light nothing can ever exist. Know ye, that in all formed matter, the heart of Light always exists. Aye, even though bound in the darkness, inherent Light always exists.

Once I stood in the Halls of Amenti and heard the voice of the Lords of Amenti, saying in tones that rang through the silence, words of power, mighty and potent. Chanted they the song of the cycles, the words that opened the path to beyond. Aye, I saw the great path opened and looked for an instant into the beyond. Saw I the movements of the cycles, vast as the thought of the Source could convey.

Knew I then that even Infinity is moving on to some unthinkable end. Saw I that the Cosmos is Order and part of a movement that extends to all space, a part of an Order of Orders, constantly moving in a harmony of space. Saw I the wheeling of cycles like vast circles across the sky. Knew I then that all that has being is growing to meet yet other being in a far-off grouping of space and of time. Knew I then that in Words are power to open the planes that are hidden from man. Aye, that even in Words lies hidden the key that will open above and below.

The Emerald Tablets

Hark ye now, man, this word I leave with thee. Use it and ye shall find power in its sound. Say ye, the word: "Zin-Uru" and power ye shall find. Yet must ye understand that man is of Light and Light is of man.

List ye, 0 man, and hear a mystery stranger than all that lies 'neath the Sun. Know ye, O man, that all space is filled by worlds within worlds; aye, one within the other yet separate by Law.

Once in my search for deep buried wisdom, I opened the door that bars Them from man. Called I from other planes of being, one who was fairer than the daughters of men. Aye, I called her from out of the spaces to shine as a Light in the world of men.

Used I the drum of the Serpent. Wore I the robe of the purple and gold. Placed on my head, I, the crown of Silver. Around me the circle of cinnabar shone. Raised I my arms and cried the invocation that opens the path to the planes beyond, cried to the Lords of the Signs in their houses: "Lords of the two horizons, watchers of the treble gates, stand ye One at the right and One at the left as the Star rises to his throne and rules over his sign. Aye, thou dark prince of Arulu, open the gates of the dim, hidden land and release her whom ye keep imprisoned. Hear ye, hear ye, hear ye, dark Lords and Shining Ones, and by their secret names, names which I know and can pronounce, hear ye and obey my will."

Lit I then with flame my circle and called Her in the space-planes beyond. "Daughter of Light return from Arulu. Seven times and seven times have I passed through the fire. Food have I not eaten. Water have I not drunk. I call thee from Arulu, from the realm of Ekershegal, I summon thee, Lady of Light."

Then before me rose the dark figures; aye, the figures of the Lords of Arulu. Parted they before me and forth came the Lady of Light.

The Key of Time

Free was she now from the Lords of the night, free to live in the Light of the earth Sun, free to live as a child of Light.

Here ye and listen, 0 my children. Magic is knowledge and only is Law. Be not afraid of the power within thee for it follows Law as the stars in the sky.

Know ye that to he without knowledge, wisdom is magic and not of the Law. But know ye that ever ye by your knowledge can approach closer to a place in the Sun.

List ye, my children, follow my teaching. Be ye ever seeker of Light. Shine in the world of men all around thee, a Light on the path that shall shine among men.

Follow ye and learn of my magic. Know that all force is thine if thou wilt. Fear not the path that leads thee to knowledge, but rather shun ye the dark road. Light is thine, O man, for the taking. Cast off the fetters and thou shalt be free.

Know ye that thy Soul is living in bondage fettered by fear that holds ye in thrall. Open thy eyes and see the great Sun-Light. Be not afraid for all is thine own. Fear is the Lord of dark Arulu to he who has never faced the dark fear. Aye, know that fear has existence created by those who are bound by their fears.

Shake off thy bondage, 0 children, and walk in the Light of the glorious day. Never turn thy thoughts to the darkness and surely ye shall be One with the Light.

Man is only what he believeth, a brother of darkness or a child of the Light. Come thou into the Light my Children. Walk in the pathway that leads to the Sun.

The Emerald Tablets

Hark ye now and list to the wisdom. Use thou the word I have given unto thee. Use it and surely thou shalt find power and wisdom and Light to walk in the way. Seek thee and find the key I have given and ever shalt thou be a Child of the Light.

EMERALD TABLET XI
The Key to Above and Below

Hear ye and list ye, O children of Khem, to the words that I give that shall bring ye to the Light. Ye know, O men, that I knew your fathers, aye, your fathers in a time long ago. Deathless have I been through all the ages, living among ye since your knowledge began. Leading ye upward to the Light of the Great Soul have I ever striven, drawing ye from out of the darkness of night.

Know ye, O people amongst whom I walk, that I, Thoth, have all of the knowledge and all of the wisdom known to man since the ancient days. Keeper have I been of the secrets of the great race, holder of the key that leads into life. Bringer up have I been to ye, O my children, even from the darkness of the Ancient of Days. List ye now to the words of my wisdom. List ye now to the message I bring. Hear ye now the words I give thee, and ye shall be raised from the darkness to Light.

Far in the past, when first I came to thee, found I thee in caves of rocks. Lifted I thee by my power and wisdom until thou didst shine as men among men. Aye, found I thee without any knowing. Only a little were ye raised beyond beasts. Fanned I ever the spark of thy consciousness until at last ye flamed as men.

Now shall I speak to thee knowledge ancient beyond the thought of thy race. Know ye that we of the Great Race had and have knowledge that is more than man's. Wisdom we gained from the star-born races, wisdom and knowledge far beyond man's. Down to us had descended the masters of wisdom as far beyond us as I am from thee.

The Emerald Tablets

List ye now while I give ye wisdom. Use it and free thou shalt be. Know ye that in the pyramid I builded are the Keys that shall show ye the Way into life. Aye, draw ye a line from the great image I builded, to the apex of the pyramid, built as a gateway. Draw ye another opposite in the same angle and direction. Dig ye and find that which I have hidden. There shall ye find the underground entrance to the secrets hidden before ye were men.

Tell ye I now of the mystery of cycles that move in movements that are strange to the finite, for infinite are they beyond knowledge of man. Know ye that there are nine of the cycles; aye, nine above and fourteen below, moving in harmony to the place of joining that shall exist in the future of time. Know ye that the Lords of the Cycles are units of consciousness sent from the others to unify This with the All. Highest are They of the consciousness of all the Cycles, working in harmony with the Law. Know They that in time all will be perfected, having none above and none below, but all One in a perfected Infinity, a harmony of all in the Oneness of All.

Deep 'neath Earth's surface in the Halls of Amenti sit the Seven, the Lords of the Cycles, aye, and another, the Lord from below. Yet know thee that in Infinity there is neither above nor below. But ever there is and ever shall be Oneness of All when all is complete. Oft have I stood before the Lords of the All. Oft at the fount of their wisdom have drunken and filled both my body and Soul with their Light.

Spake they to me and told me of cycles and the Law that gives them the means to exist. Aye, spake to me the Lord of the Nine saying: "O, Thoth, great are ye among Earth's children, but mysteries exist of which ye know not. Ye know that ye came from a space-time below this and know ye shall travel to a space-time beyond. But little ye know of the mysteries within them, little ye

The Key to Above and Below

know of the wisdom beyond. Know ye that ye as a whole in this consciousness are only a cell in the process of growth. The consciousness below thee is ever-expanding in different ways from those known to thee. Aye, it, though in space-time below thee, is ever growing in ways that are different from those that were part of the ways of thine own. For know that it grows as a result of thy growth but not in the same way that thou didst grow. The growth that thou had and have in the present have brought into being a cause and effect.

No consciousness follows the path of those before it, else all would be repetition and vain. Each consciousness in the cycle it exists in follows its own path to the ultimate goal. Each plays its part in the Plan of the Cosmos. Each plays its part in the ultimate end. The farther the cycle, the greater its knowledge and ability to blend the Law of the whole. Know ye, that ye in the cycles below us are working the minor parts of the Law, while we of the cycle that extends to Infinity take of the striving and build greater Law.

Each has his own part to play in the cycles. Each has his work to complete in his way. The cycle below thee is yet not below thee but only formed for a need that exists. For know ye that the fountain of wisdom that sends forth the cycles is eternally seeking new powers to gain. Ye know that knowledge is gained only by practice, and wisdom comes forth only from knowledge, and thus are the cycles created by Law. Means are they for the gaining of knowledge for the Plane of Law that is the Source of the All.

The cycle below is not truly below but only different in space and in time. The consciousness there is working and testing lesser things than those ye are. And know, just as ye are working on greater, so above ye are those who are also working as ye are on

The Emerald Tablets

yet other laws. The difference that exists between the cycles is only in ability to work with the Law.

We, who have being in cycles beyond thee, are those who first came forth from the Source and have in the passage through time-space gained ability to use Laws of the Greater that are far beyond the conception of man. Nothing there is that is really below thee but only a different operation of Law.

Look thee above or look thee below, the same shall ye find. For all is but part of the Oneness that is at the Source of the Law. The consciousness below thee is part thine own as we are a part of thine.

Ye, as a child had not the knowledge that came to ye when ye became a man. Compare ye the cycles to man in his journey from birth unto death, and see in the cycle below thee the child with the knowledge he has; and see ye yourself as the child grown older, advancing in knowledge as time passes on. See ye, We, also, the child grown to manhood with the knowledge and wisdom that came with the years.

So also, O Thoth, are the cycles of consciousness, children in different stages of growth, yet all from the one Source, the Wisdom, and all to the Wisdom returning again." Ceased then He from speaking and sat in the silence that comes to the Lords.

Then again spake He unto me, saying: "O Thoth, long have We sat in Amenti, guarding the flame of life in the Halls. Yet know, we are still part of our Cycles with our Vision reaching unto them and beyond. Aye, know we that of all, nothing else matters excepting the growth we can gain with our Soul. Know we the flesh is fleeting. The things men count great are nothing to us. The things we seek are not of the body but are only the perfected state of the

The Key to Above and Below

Soul. When ye as men can learn that nothing but progress of Soul can count in the end, then truly ye are free from all bondage, free to work in a harmony of Law.

Know, 0 man, ye should aim at perfection, for only thus can ye attain to the goal. Though ye should know that nothing is perfect, yet it should be thy aim and thy goal." Ceased again the voice of the Nine, and into my consciousness the words had sunk.

Now, seek I ever more wisdom that I may be perfect in Law with the All.

Soon go I down to the Halls of Amenti to live 'neath the cold flower of life. Ye whom I have taught shall nevermore see me. Yet live I forever in the wisdom I taught.

All that man is is because of his wisdom. All that he shall be is the result of his cause.

List ye, now to my voice and become greater than common man. Lift thine eyes upward, let Light fill thy being, be thou ever Children of Light. Only by effort shall ye grow upward to the plane where Light is the All of the All. Be ye the master of all that surrounds thee. Never be mastered by the effects of thy life. Create then ever more perfect causes and in time shalt thou be a Sun of the Light.

Free, let thine soul soar ever upward, free from the bondage and fetters of night. Lift thine eyes to the Sun in the sky-space. For thee, let it be a symbol of life. Know that thou art the Greater Light, perfect in thine own sphere, when thou art free. Look not ever into the blackness. Lift up thine eyes to the space above. Free let thine Light flame upward and shalt thou be a Child of the Light.

EMERALD TABLET XII
The Law of Cause and Effect & The Key of Prophecy

List ye, 0 man, to the words of my wisdom, list to the voice of Thoth, the Atlantean. Conquered have I the Law of time-space. Knowledge have I gained of the future of time.

Know I that man in his movement through space-time shall ever be One with the All. Know ye, O man, that all of the future is an open book to him who can read. All effect shall bring forth its causes as all effects grew from the first cause.

Know ye the future is not fixed or stable but varies as cause brings forth an effect. Look in the cause thou shalt bring into being, and surely thou shalt see that all is effect.

So, 0 man, be sure the effects that ye bring forth are ever causes of more perfect effects. Know ye the future is never in fixation but follows man's free will as it moves through the movements of time-space toward the goal where a new time begins. Man can only read the future through the causes that bring the effects. Seek ye within the causation and surely ye shall find the effects.

List ye, 0 man, while I speak of the future, speak of the effect that follows the cause. Know ye that man in his journey light-ward is ever seeking escape from the night that surrounds him, like the shadows that surround the stars in the sky and like the stars in the sky-space, he, too, shall shine from the shadows of night.

Ever his destiny shall lead him onward until he is One with the Light. Aye, though his way lies midst the shadows, ever before

The Law of Cause and Effect and The Key of Prophecy

him glows the Great Light. Dark though the way be yet shall he conquer the shadows that flow around him like night.

Far in the future, I see man as Light-born, free from the darkness that fetters the Soul, living in Light without the bounds of the darkness to cover the Light that is Light of their Soul. Know ye, 0 man, before ye attain this that many the dark shadows shall fall on your Light striving to quench with the shadows of darkness the Light of the Soul that strives to be free.

Great is the struggle between Light and darkness, age old and yet ever new. Yet, know in a time, far in the future, Light shall be All and darkness shall fall. List ye, O man, to my words of wisdom. Prepare and ye shall not bind your Light. Man has risen and man has fallen as ever new waves of consciousness flow from the great abyss below us toward the Sun of their goal.

Ye, my children, have risen from a state that was little above the beast, until now of all men ye are greatest. Yet before thee were others greater than thee. Yet tell I thee as before thee others have fallen, so also shall ye come to an end. And upon the land where ye dwell now, barbarians shall dwell and in turn rise to Light.

Forgotten shall be the ancient-wisdom, yet ever shall live though hidden from men. Aye, in the land thou callest Khem, races shall rise and races shall fall. Forgotten shalt thou be of the children of men. Yet thou shalt have moved to a star-space beyond this leaving behind this place where thou has dwelt.

The Soul of man moves ever onward, bound not by any one star. But ever moving to the great goal before him where he is dissolved in the Light of the All. Know ye that ye shall ever go onward, moved by the Law of cause and effect until in the end both become One.

The Emerald Tablets

Aye, man, after ye have gone, others shall move in the places ye lived. Knowledge and wisdom shall all be forgotten, and only a memory of Gods shall survive. As I to thee am a God by my knowledge, so ye, too shall be Gods of the future because of your knowledge far above theirs. Yet know ye that all through the ages, man shall have access to Law when he will.

Ages to come shall see revival of wisdom to those who shall inherit thy place on this star. They shall, in turn, come into wisdom and learn to banish the darkness by Light.

Yet greatly must they strive through the ages to bring unto themselves the freedom of Light. Then shall there come unto man the great warfare that shall make the Earth tremble and shake in its course. Aye, then shall the Dark Brothers open the warfare between Light and the night.

When man again shall conquer the ocean and fly in the air on wings like the birds; when he has learned to harness the lightning, then shall the time of warfare begin.

Great shall the battle be twixt the forces, great the warfare of darkness and Light. Nation shall rise against nation using the dark forces to shatter the Earth.

Weapons of force shall wipe out the Earth-man until half of the races of men shall be gone. Then shall come forth the Sons of the Morning and give their edict to the children of men, saying: "0 men, cease from thy striving against thy brother. Only thus can ye come to the Light. Cease from thy unbelief, 0 my brother, and follow the path and know ye are right."

Then shall men cease from their striving, brother against brother and father against son.

The Law of Cause and Effect and The Key of Prophecy

Then shall the ancient home of my people rise from its place 'neath the dark ocean waves.

Then shall the Age of Light be unfolded with all men seeking the Light of the goal.

Then shall the Brothers of Light rule the people. Banished shall be the darkness of night. Aye, the children of men shall progress onward and upward to the great goal.

Children of Light shall they become. Flame of the flame shall their Souls ever be. Knowledge and wisdom shall be man's in the great age for he shall approach the eternal flame, the Source of all wisdom, the place of beginning, that is yet One with the end of all things. Aye, in a time that is yet unborn, all shall be One and One shall be All. Man, a perfect flame of this Cosmos, shall move forward to a place in the stars. Aye, shall move even from out of this space-time into another beyond the stars.

Long have ye listened to me, O my children, long have ye listened to the wisdom of Thoth. Now I depart from ye into darkness. Now go I to the Halls of Amenti, there to dwell in the future when Light shall come again to man. Yet, know ye, my Spirit shall ever be with thee, guiding thy feet in the pathway of Light.

Guard ye the secrets I leave with thee, and surely my spirit will guard thee through life. Keep thine eyes ever on the pathway to wisdom. Keep the Light as thy goal evermore. Fetter not thy Soul in bondage of darkness; free let it wing in its flight to the stars.

Now I depart thee to dwell in Amenti. Be thou my children in this life and the next. The time will come when ye, too, shall be deathless, living from age to age a Light among men.

The Emerald Tablets

Guard ye the entrance to the Halls of Amenti. Guard ye the secrets I have hidden among ye. Let not the wisdom be cast to barbarians. Secret shall thou keep it for those who seek Light. Now depart I. Receive thou my blessing. Take thou my way and follow the Light.

Blend thou thy Soul in the Great Essence. One, with the Great Light let thy consciousness be. Call thou on me when thou dost need me. Use my name three times in a row:

EMERALD TABLET XIII
The Keys of Life and Death

List ye, 0 man, hear ye the wisdom. Hear ye the Word that shall fill thee with Life. Hear ye the Word that shall banish the darkness. Hear ye the voice that shall banish the night.

Mystery and wisdom have I brought to my children; knowledge and power descended from old. Know ye not that all shall be opened when ye shall find the oneness of all? One shall ye be with the Masters of Mystery, Conquerors of Death and Masters of Life. Aye, ye shall learn of the flower of Amenti the blossom of life that shines in the Halls. In Spirit shall ye reach that Halls of Amenti and bring back the wisdom that liveth in Light.

Know ye the gateway to power is secret.

Know ye the gateway to life is through death. Aye, through death but not as ye know death, but a death that is life and is fire and is Light. Desireth thou to know the deep, hidden secret? Look in thy heart where the knowledge is bound.

Know that in thee the secret is hidden, the source of all life and the source of all death.

List ye, O man, while I tell the secret, reveal unto thee the secret of old. Deep in Earth's heart lies the flower, the source of the Spirit that binds all in its form. For know ye that the Earth is living in body as thou art alive in thine own formed form.

The Flower of Life is as thine own place of Spirit and streams through the Earth as thine flows through thy form; giving of life to the Earth and its children, renewing the Spirit from form unto form. This is the Spirit that is form of thy body, shaping and moulding into its form.

Know ye, 0 man, that thy form is dual, balanced in polarity while formed in its form.

Know that when fast on thee Death approaches, it is only because thy balance is shaken. It is only because one pole has been lost.

Know that thy body when in perfect balance may never be touched by the finger of Death. Aye, even accident may only approach when the balance is gone. When ye are in a balanced equilibrium, ye shall live on in time and not taste of Death.

Know that thou art the balanced completion, existing because of thy balance of poles. As, in thee, one pole is drawn downward, fast from thee goes the balance of life. Then unto thee cold Death approaches, and change must come to thine unbalanced life.

Know that the secret of life in Amenti is the secret of restoring the balance of poles. All that exists has form and is living because of the Spirit of life in its poles. See ye not that in Earth's heart is the balance of all things that exist and have being on its face? The source of thy Spirit is drawn from Earth's heart, for in thy form thou are one with the Earth.

When thou hast learned to hold thine own balance, then shalt thou draw on the balance of Earth. Exist then shalt thou while Earth is existing, changing in form, only when Earth, too, shalt change: Tasting not of death, but one with this planet, holding thy form till all pass away.

List ye, O man, whilst I give the secret so that ye, too, shalt taste not of change. One hour each day shalt thou lie with thine head pointed to the place of the positive pole (north). One hour each day

The Keys of Life and Death

shalt thy head be pointed to the place of the negative pole (south). Whilst thy head is placed to the northward, hold thou thy consciousness from the chest to the head. And when thy head is placed southward, hold thou thy thought from chest to the feet. Hold thou in balance once in each seven, and thy balance will retain the whole of its strength. Aye, if thou be old, thy body will freshen and thy strength will become as a youth's. This is the secret known to the Masters by which they hold off the fingers of Death. Neglect not to follow the path I have shown, for when thou hast passed beyond years to a hundred to neglect it will mean the coming of Death.

Hear ye, my words, and follow the pathway. Keep thou thy balance and live on in life.

Hear ye, O man, and list to my voice. List to the wisdom that gives thee of Death. When at the end of thy work appointed, thou may desire to pass from this life, pass to the plane where the Suns of the Morning live and have being as Children of Light. Pass without pain and pass without sorrow into the plane where is eternal Light.

First lie at rest with thine head to the eastward. Fold thou thy hands at the Source of thy life (solar plexus). Place thou thy consciousness in the life seat. Whirl it and divide to north and to south. Send thou the one out toward the northward. Send thou the other out to the south. Relax thou thy hold upon thy being. Forth from they form will thy silver spark fly, upward and onward to the Sun of the morning, blending with Light, at one with its source. There it shall flame till desire shall be created. Then shall return to a place in a form.

Know ye, 0 men, that thus pass the great Souls, changing at will from life unto life. Thus ever passes the Avatar, willing his Death as he wills his own life.

List ye, O man, drink of my wisdom. Learn ye the secret that is Master of Time. Learn ye how those ye call Masters are able to remember the lives of the past. Great is the secret yet easy to master, giving to thee the mastery of time. When upon thee death fast approaches, fear not but know ye are master of Death. Relax thy body, resist not with tension. Place in thy heart the flame of thy Soul. Swiftly then sweep it to the seat of the triangle. Hold for a moment, then move to the goal. This, thy goal, is the place between thine eyebrows, the place where the memory of life must hold sway. Hold thou thy flame here in thy brain-seat until the fingers of Death grasp thy Soul.

Then as thou pass through the state of transition, surely the memories of life shall pass, too. Then shalt the past be as one with the present. Then shall the memory of all be retained. Free shalt thou be from all retrogression. The things of the past shall live in today.

Supplementary EMERALD TABLET XIV

Atlantis

List ye, O Man, to the deep hidden wisdom, lost to the world since the time of the Dwellers, lost and forgotten by men of this age.

Know ye this Earth is but a portal, guarded by powers unknown to man. Yet, the Dark Lords hide the entrance that leads to the Heaven-born land. Know ye, the way to the sphere of Arulu is guarded by barriers opened only to Light-born man.

Upon Earth, I am the holder of the keys to the gates of the Sacred Land. Command I, by the powers beyond me, to leave the keys to the world of man. Before I depart, I give ye the Secrets of how ye may rise from the bondage of darkness, cast off the fetters of flesh that have bound ye, rise from the darkness into the Light.

Know ye, the soul must be cleansed of its darkness, ere ye may enter the portals of Light. Thus, I established among ye the Mysteries so that the Secrets may always be found. Aye, though man may fall into darkness, always the Light will shine as a guide. Hidden in darkness, veiled in symbols, always the way to the portal will be found. Man in the future will deny the mysteries but always the way the seeker will find.

Now I command ye to maintain my secrets, giving only to those ye have tested, so that the pure may not be corrupted, so that the power of Truth may prevail. List ye now to the unveiling of Mystery. List to the symbols of Mystery I give. Make of it a religion for only thus will its essence remain.

The Emerald Tablets

Regions there are two between this life and the Great One, traveled by the Souls who depart from this Earth; Duat, the home of the powers of illusion; Sekhet Hetspet, the House of the Gods. Osiris, the symbol of the guard of the portal, who turns back the souls of unworthy men. Beyond lies the sphere of the heaven-born powers, Arulu, the land where the Great Ones have passed. There, when my work among men has been finished, will I join the Great Ones of my Ancient home.

Seven are the mansions of the house of the Mighty; Three guards the portal of each house from the darkness; Fifteen the ways that lead to Duat. Twelve are the houses of the Lords of Illusion, facing four ways, each of them different. Forty and Two are the great powers, judging the Dead who seek for the portal. Four are the Sons of Horus, Two are the Guards of East and West— I sis, the mother who pleads for her children, Queen of the moon, reflecting the Sun. Ba is the essence, living forever. Ka is the Shadow that man knows as life. Ba cometh not until Ka is incarnate. These are mysteries to preserve through the ages. Keys are they of life and of Death.

Hear ye now the mystery of mysteries: learn of the circle beginningless and endless, the form of He who is One and in all.

Listen and hear it, go forth and apply it, thus will ye travel the way that I go. Mystery in Mystery, yet clear to the Light-born, the Secret of all I now will reveal. I will declare a secret to the initiated, but let the door be wholly shut against the profane.

Three is the mystery, come from the great one. Hear, and Light on thee will dawn. In the primeval, dwell three unities. Other than these, none can exist. These are the equilibrium, source of creation: one God, one Truth, one point of freedom.

Atlantis

Three come forth from the three of the balance: all life, all good, all power.

Three are the qualities of God in his Light-home: Infinite power, Infinite Wisdom, Infinite Love.

Three are the powers given to the Masters: To transmute evil, assist good, use discrimination.

Three are the things inevitable for God to perform: Manifest power, wisdom and love.

Three are the powers creating all things: Divine Love possessed of perfect knowledge, Divine Wisdom knowing all possible means, Divine Power possessed by the joint will of Divine Love and Wisdom.

Three are the circles (states) of existence: The circle of Light where dwells nothing but God, and only God can traverse it; the circle of Chaos where all things by nature arise from death; the Circle of awareness where all things spring from life.

All things animate are of three states of existence: chaos or death, liberty in humanity and felicity of Heaven.

Three necessities control all things: beginning in the Great Deep, the circle of chaos, plenitude in Heaven.

Three are the paths of the Soul: Man, Liberty, Light.

Three are the hindrances: lack of endeavor to obtain knowledge; non-attachment to god; attachment to evil.

In man, the three are manifest. Three are the Kings of power within. Three are the chambers of the mysteries, found yet not found in the body of man.

The Emerald Tablets

Hear ye now of he who is liberated, freed from the bondage of life into Light. Knowing the source of all worlds shall be open. Aye, even the Gates of Arulu shall not be barred. Yet heed, O man, who wouldst enter heaven. If ye be not worthy, better it be to fall into the fire.

Know ye the celestials pass through the pure flame. At every revolution of the heavens, they bathe in the fountains of Light.

List ye, 0 man, to this mystery: Long in the past before ye were man- born, I dwelled in Ancient Atlantis. There in the Temple, I drank of the Wisdom, poured as a fountain of Light from the Dweller. Give the key to ascend to the Presence of Light in the Great world. Stood I before the Holy One enthroned in the flower of fire. Veiled was he by the lightnings of darkness, else my Soul by the Glory have been shattered.

Forth from the feet of his Throne like the diamond, rolled forth four rivers of flame from his footstool, rolled through the channels of clouds to the Man-world. Filled was the hall with Spirits of Heaven. Wonder of wonders was the Starry palace. Above the sky, like a rainbow of Fire and Sunlight, were formed the spirits. Sang they the glories of the Holy One.

Then from the midst of the Fire came a voice: "Behold the Glory of the first Cause." I beheld that Light, high above all darkness, reflected in my own being. I attained, as it were, to the God of all Gods, the Spirit-Sun, the Sovereign of the Sun spheres.

Again came the Voice: "There is one, even the First, who hath no beginning, who hath no end; who hath made all things, who govern all, who is good, who is just, who illumines, who sustains."

Atlantis

Then from the throne, there poured a great radiance, surrounding and lifting my soul by its power. Swiftly I moved through the spaces of Heaven, shown was I the mystery of mysteries, shown the Secret heart of the cosmos. Carried was I to the land of Arulu, stood before the Lords in their Houses.

Opened they the Doorway so I might glimpse the primeval chaos. Shuddered my soul to the vision of horror, shrank back my soul from the ocean of darkness. Then saw I the need for the barriers, saw the need for the Lords of Arulu. Only they with their Infinite balance could stand in the way of the inpouring chaos.

Only they could guard God's creation.

Then did I pass 'round the circle of eight. Saw all the souls who had conquered the darkness. Saw the splendor of Light where they dwelled. Longed I to take my place in their circle, but longed I also for the way I had chosen, when I stood in the Halls of Amenti and made my choice to the work I would do.

Passed I from the Halls of Arulu down to the earth space where my body lay. Arose I from the earth where I rested. Stood I before the Dweller. Gave my pledge to renounce my Great right until my work on Earth was completed, until the Age of darkness be past.

List ye, 0 man, to the words I shall give ye. In them shall ye find the Essence of Life. Before I return to the Halls of Amenti, taught shall ye be the Secrets of Secrets, how ye, too, may arise to the Light. Preserve them and guard them, hide them in symbols, so the profane will laugh and renounce. In every land, form ye the mysteries. Make the way hard for the seeker to tread. Thus will the weak and the wavering be rejected. Thus will the secrets be hidden and guarded, held till the time when the wheel shall be turned.

The Emerald Tablets

Through the dark ages, waiting and watching, my Spirit shall remain in the deep hidden land. When one has passed all the trials of the outer, summon ye me by the Key that ye hold. Then will I, the Initiator, answer, come from the Halls of the Gods in Amenti. Then will I receive the initiate, give him the words of power.

Hark ye, remember, these words of warning: bring not to me one lacking in wisdom, impure in heart or weak in his purpose. Else I will withdraw from ye your power to summon me from the place of my sleeping.

Go forth and conquer the element of darkness. Exalt in thy nature thine essence of Light.

Now go ye forth and summon thy brothers so that I may impart the wisdom to light thy path when my presence is gone. Come to the chamber beneath my temple. Eat not food until three days are past. There will I give thee the essence of wisdom so that with power ye may shine amongst men. There will I give unto thee the secrets so that ye, to , may rise to the Heavens — God men in Truth as in essence ye be.

Depart now and leave me while I summon those ye know of but as yet know not.

Supplementary EMERALD TABLET XV

Secret of Secrets

Now ye assemble, my children, waiting to hear the Secret of Secrets which shall give ye power to unfold the God-man, give ye the way to Eternal life. Plainly shall I speak of the Unveiled Mysteries. No dark sayings shall I give unto thee. Open thine ears now, my children. Hear and obey the words that I give.

First I shall speak of the fetters of darkness which bind ye in chains to the sphere of the Earth.

Darkness and light are both of one nature, different only in seeming, for each arose from the source of all. Darkness is disorder. Light is Order. Darkness transmuted is light of the Light. This, my children, your purpose in being; transmutation of darkness to light

Hear ye now of the mystery of nature, the relations of life to the Earth where it dwells. Know ye, ye are threefold in nature, physical, astral and mental in one.

Three are the qualities of each of the natures; nine in all, as above, so below. In the physical are these channels, the blood which moves in vortical motion, reacting on the heart to continue its beating. Magnetism which moves through the nerve paths, carrier of energies to all cells and tissues. Akasa which flows through channels, subtle yet physical, completing the channels. Each of the three attuned with each other, each affecting the life of the body. Form they the skeletal framework through which the subtle ether flows. In their mastery lies the Secret of Life in the body.

The Emerald Tablets

Relinquished only by will of the adept, when his purpose in living is done.

Three are the natures of the Astral, mediator is between above and below; not of the physical, not of the Spiritual, but able to move above and below.

Three are the natures of Mind, carrier it of the Will of the Great One. Arbitrator of Cause and Effect in thy life. Thus is formed the threefold being, directed from above by the power of four. Above and beyond man's threefold nature lies the realm of the Spiritual Self.

Four is it in qualities, shining in each of the planes of existence, but thirteen in one, the mystical number. Based on the qualities of man are the Brothers: each shall direct the unfoldment of being, each shall channels be of the Great One.

On Earth, man is in bondage, bound by space and time to the earth plane. Encircling each planet, a wave of vibration, binds him to his plane of unfoldment. Yet within man is the Key to releasement, within man may freedom be found.

When ye have released the self from the body, rise to the outermost bounds of your earth-plane. Speak ye the word Dor-E-Lil-La. Then for a time your Light will be lifted, free may ye pass the barriers of space. For a time of half of the sun (six hours), free may ye pass the barriers of earth- plane, see and know those who are beyond thee. Yea, to the highest worlds may ye pass. See your own possible heights of unfoldment, know all earthly futures of Soul.

Bound are ye in your body, but by the power ye may be free. This is the Secret whereby bondage shall be replaced by freedom for thee.

Secret of Secrets

Calm let thy mind be. At rest be thy body: Conscious only of freedom from flesh.

Center thy being on the goal of thy longing. Think over and over that thou wouldst be free. Think of this word— La-Um-I-L-Gan— over and over in thy mind let it sound. Drift with the sound to the place of thy longing. Free from the bondage of flesh by thy will.

Hear ye while I give the greatest of secrets: how ye may enter the Halls of Amenti, enter the place of the immortals as I did, stand before the Lords in their places.

Lie ye down in rest of thy body. Calm thy mind so no thought disturbs thee. Pure must ye be in mind and in purpose, else only failure will come unto thee. Vision Amenti as I have told in my Tablets. Long with fullness of heart to be there. Stand before the Lords in thy mind's eye. Pronounce the words of power I give (mentally); Mekut-EI-Shab- El Hale-Sur-Ben-EI-Zabrut Zin-Efrim-Quar-EI. Relax thy mind and thy body. Then be sure your soul will be called.

Now give I the Key to Shamballa, the place where my Brothers live in the darkness: Darkness but filled with Light of the Sun— Darkness of Earth, but Light of the Spirit, guides for ye when my day is done.

Leave thou thy body as I have taught thee. Pass to the barriers of the deep, hidden place. Stand before the gates and their guardians. Command thy entrance by these words: "I am the Light. In me is no darkness. Free am I of the bondage of night. Open thou the way of the Twelve and the One, so I may pass to the realm of wisdom."

When they refuse thee, as surely they will, command them to open by these words of power: "I am the Light. For me are no barriers.

The Emerald Tablets

Open, I command, by the Secret of Secrets— Edom-EI-Ahim-Sabbert-Zur Adorn."

Then if thy words have been "Truth" of the highest, open for thee the barriers will fall.

Now, I leave thee, my children. Down, yet up, to the Halls shall I go. Win ye the way to me, my children. Truly my brothers shall ye become.

Thus finish I my writings. Keys let them be to those who come after. But only to those who seek my wisdom, for only for these am I the Key and the Way.

The Kybalion

By Three Initiates

INTRODUCTION

We take great pleasure in presenting to the attention of students and investigators of the Secret Doctrines this little work based upon the world-old Hermetic Teachings. There has been so little written upon this subject, not withstanding the countless references to the Teachings in the many works upon occultism, that the many earnest searchers after the Arcane Truths will doubtless welcome the appearance of this present volume.

The purpose of this work is not the enunciation of any special philosophy or doctrine, but rather is to give to the students a statement of the Truth that will serve to reconcile the many bits of occult knowledge that they may have acquired, but which are apparently opposed to each other and which often serve to discourage and disgust the beginner in the study. Our intent is not to erect a new Temple of Knowledge, but rather to place in the hands of the student a Master-Key with which he may open the many inner doors in the Temple of Mystery through the main portals he has already entered.

There is no portion of the occult teachings possessed by the world which have been so closely guarded as the fragments of the Hermetic Teachings which have come down to us over the tens of centuries which have elapsed since the lifetime of its great founder, Hermes Trismegistus, the "scribe of the gods," who dwelt in old Egypt in the days when the present race of men was in its infancy. Contemporary with Abraham, and, if the legends be true, an instructor of that venerable sage, Hermes was, and is, the Great Central Sun of Occultism, whose rays have served to illumine the countless teachings which have been promulgated since his time. All the fundamental and basic teachings embedded in the esoteric teachings of every race may be traced back to Hermes. Even the most ancient teachings of India undoubtedly have their roots in the original Hermetic Teachings.

From the land of the Ganges many advanced occultists wandered to the land of Egypt, and sat at the feet of the Master. From him they obtained the Master-Key which explained and reconciled their divergent views, and thus the Secret Doctrine was firmly established. From other lands also came the learned ones, all of whom regarded Hermes as the Master of Masters, and his influence was so great that in spite of the many wanderings from the path on the part of the centuries of teachers in these different lands, there may still be found a certain basic resemblance and correspondence which underlies the many and often quite divergent theories entertained and taught by the occultists of these different lands today. The student of Comparative Religions will be able to perceive the influence of the Hermetic Teachings in every religion worthy of the name, now known to man, whether it be a dead religion or one in full vigor in our own times. There is always certain correspondence in spite of the contradictory features, and the Hermetic Teachings act as the Great Reconciler.

The lifework of Hermes seems to have been in the direction of planting the great Seed-Truth which has grown and blossomed in so many strange forms, rather than to establish a school of philosophy which would dominate, the world's thought. But, nevertheless, the original truths taught by him have been kept intact in their original purity by a few men each age, who, refusing great numbers of half-developed students and followers, followed the Hermetic custom and reserved their truth for the few who were ready to comprehend and master it. From lip to ear the truth has been handed down among the few. There have always been a few Initiates in each generation, in the various lands of the earth, who kept alive the sacred flame of the Hermetic Teachings, and such have always been willing to use their lamps to re-light the lesser

Introduction

lamps of the outside world, when the light of truth grew dim, and clouded by reason of neglect, and when the wicks became clogged with foreign matter. There were always a few to tend faithfully the altar of the Truth, upon which was kept alight the Perpetual Lamp of Wisdom. These men devoted their lives to the labor of love which the poet has so well stated in his lines:

"O, let not the flame die out! Cherished age after age in its dark cavern--in its holy temples cherished. Fed by pure ministers of love--let not the flame die out!"

These men have never sought popular approval, nor numbers of followers. They are indifferent to these things, for they know how few there are in each generation who are ready for the truth, or who would recognize it if it were presented to them. They reserve the "strong meat for men," while others furnish the "milk for babes." They reserve their pearls of wisdom for the few elect, who recognize their value and who wear them in their crowns, instead of casting them before the materialistic vulgar swine, who would trample them in the mud and mix them with their disgusting mental food. But still these men have never forgotten or overlooked the original teachings of Hermes, regarding the passing on of the words of truth to those ready to receive it, which teaching is stated in The Kybalion as follows: "Where fall the footsteps of the Master, the ears of those ready for his Teaching open wide." And again: "When the ears of the student are ready to hear, then cometh the lips to fill them with wisdom." But their customary attitude has always been strictly in accordance with the other Hermetic aphorism, also in The Kybalion: "The lips of Wisdom are closed, except to the ears of Understanding."

There are those who have criticized this attitude of the Hermetists, and who have claimed that they did not manifest the proper spirit in their policy of seclusion and reticence. But a moment's glance back over the pages of history will show the wisdom of the

Masters, who knew the folly of attempting to teach to the world that which it was neither ready or willing to receive. The Hermetists have never sought to be martyrs, and have, instead, sat silently aside with a pitying smile on their closed lips, while the "heathen raged noisily about them" in their customary amusement of putting to death and torture the honest but misguided enthusiasts who imagined that they could force upon a race of barbarians the truth capable of being understood only by the elect who had advanced along The Path.

And the spirit of persecution has not as yet died out in the land. There are certain Hermetic Teachings, which, if publicly promulgated, would bring down upon the teachers a great cry of scorn and revilement from the multitude, who would again raise the cry of "Crucify! Crucify."

In this little work we have endeavored to give you an idea of the fundamental teachings of The Kybalion, striving to give you the working Principles, leaving you to apply therm yourselves, rather than attempting to work out the teaching in detail. If you are a true student, you will be able to work out and apply these Principles-- if not, then you must develop yourself into one, for otherwise the Hermetic Teachings will be as "words, words, words" to you.

THE THREE INITIATES.

CHAPTER I

THE HERMETIC PHILOSOPHY

"The lips of wisdom are closed, except to the ears of Understanding"--The Kybalion.

From old Egypt have come the fundamental esoteric and occult teachings which have so strongly influenced the philosophies of all races, nations and peoples, for several thousand years. Egypt, the home of the Pyramids and the Sphinx, was the birthplace of the Hidden Wisdom and Mystic Teachings. From her Secret Doctrine all nations have borrowed. India, Persia, Chaldea, Medea, China, Japan, Assyria, ancient Greece and Rome, and other ancient countries partook liberally at the feast of knowledge which the Hierophants and Masters of the Land of Isis so freely provided for those who came prepared to partake of the great store of Mystic and Occult Lore which the masterminds of that ancient land had gathered together.

In ancient Egypt dwelt the great Adepts and Masters who have never been surpassed, and who seldom have been equaled, during the centuries that have taken their processional flight since the days of the Great Hermes. In Egypt was located the Great Lodge of Lodges of the Mystics. At the doors of her Temples entered the Neophytes who afterward, as Hierophants, Adepts, and Masters, traveled to the four corners of the earth, carrying with them the precious knowledge which they were ready, anxious, and willing to pass on to those who were ready to receive the same. All students of the Occult recognize the debt that they owe to these venerable Masters of that ancient land.

But among these great Masters of Ancient Egypt there once dwelt one of whom Masters hailed as "The Master of Masters." This man, if "man" indeed he was, dwelt in Egypt in the earliest days. He was

The Kybalion

known as Hermes Trismegistus. He was the father of the Occult Wisdom; the founder of Astrology; the discoverer of Alchemy. The details of his life story are lost to history, owing to the lapse of the years, though several of the ancient countries disputed with each other in their claims to the honor of having furnished his birthplace--and this thousands of years ago. The date of his sojourn in Egypt, in that his last incarnation on this planet, is not now known, but it has been fixed at the early days of the oldest dynasties of Egypt--long before the days of Moses. The best authorities regard him as a contemporary of Abraham, and some of the Jewish traditions go so far as to claim that Abraham acquired a portion of his mystic knowledge from Hermes himself.

As the years rolled by after his passing from this plane of life (tradition recording that he lived three hundred years in the flesh), the Egyptians deified Hermes, and made him one of their gods, under the name of Thoth. Years after, the people of Ancient Greece also made him one of their many gods--calling him "Hermes, the god of Wisdom." The Egyptians revered his memory for many centuries-yes, tens of centuries-- calling him "the Scribe of the Gods," and bestowing upon him, distinctively, his ancient title, "Trismegistus," which means "the thrice-great"; "the great-great"; "the greatest-great"; etc. In all the ancient lands, the name of Hermes Trismegistus was revered, the name being synonymous with the "Fount of Wisdom."

Even to this day, we use the term "hermetic" in the sense of "secret"; "sealed so that nothing can escape"; etc., and this by reason of the fact that the followers of Hermes always observed the principle of secrecy in their teachings. They did not believe in "casting pearls before swine," but rather held to the teaching "milk for babes"; "meat for strong men," both of which maxims are familiar to readers of the Christian scriptures, but both of which had been used by the Egyptians for centuries before the Christian era.

Hermetic Philosophy

And this policy of careful dissemination of the truth has always characterized the Hermetics, even unto the present day. The Hermetic Teachings are to be found in all lands, among all religions, but never identified with any particular country, nor with any particular religious sect. This because of the warning of the ancient teachers against allowing the Secret Doctrine to become crystallized into a creed. The wisdom of this caution is apparent to all students of history. The ancient occultism of India and Persia degenerated, and was largely lost, owing to the fact that the teachers became priests, and so mixed theology with the philosophy, the result being that the occultism of India and Persia has been gradually lost amidst the mass of religious superstition, cults, creeds and "gods." So it was with Ancient Greece and Rome. So it was with the Hermetic Teachings of the Gnostics and Early Christians, which were lost at the time of Constantine, whose iron hand smothered philosophy with the blanket of theology, losing to the Christian Church that which was its very essence and spirit, and causing it to grope throughout several centuries before it found the way back to its ancient faith, the indications apparent to all careful observers in this Twentieth Century being that the Church is now struggling to get back to its ancient mystic teachings.

But there were always a few faithful souls who kept alive the Flame, tending it carefully, and not allowing its light to become extinguished. And thanks to these staunch hearts, and fearless minds, we have the truth still with us. But it is not found in books, to any great extent. It has been passed along from Master to Student; from Initiate to Hierophant; from lip to ear. When it was written down at all, its meaning was veiled in terms of alchemy and astrology so that only those possessing the key could read it aright. This was made necessary in order to avoid the persecutions of the theologians of the Middle Ages, who fought the Secret Doctrine with fire and sword; stake, gibbet and cross. Even to this day there will be found but few reliable books on the Hermetic Philosophy, although there are countless references to it in many books written on various phases of Occultism. And yet, the Hermetic Philosophy is the only Master Key which will open all the doors of the Occult Teachings!

In the early days, there was a compilation of certain Basic Hermetic Doctrines, passed on from teacher to student, which was known as "THE KYBALION," the exact significance and meaning of the term having been lost for several centuries. This teaching, however, is known to many to whom it has descended, from mouth to ear, on and on throughout the centuries. Its precepts have never been written down, or printed, so far as we know. It was merely a collection of maxims, axioms, and precepts, which were non-understandable to outsiders, but which were readily understood by students, after the axioms, maxims, and precepts had been explained and exemplified by the Hermetic Initiates to their Neophytes. These teachings really constituted the basic principles of "The Art of Hermetic Alchemy," which, contrary to the general belief, dealt in the mastery of Mental Forces, rather than Material Elements-the Transmutation of one kind of Mental Vibrations into others, instead of the changing of one kind of metal into another. The legends of the "Philosopher's Stone" which would turn base metal into Gold, was an allegory relating to Hermetic Philosophy, readily understood by all students of true Hermeticism.

In this little book, of which this is the First Lesson, we invite our students to examine into the Hermetic Teachings, as set forth in THE KYBALION, and as explained by ourselves, humble students of the Teachings, who, while bearing the title of Initiates, are still students at the feet of HERMES, the Master. We herein give you many of the maxims, axioms and precepts of THE KYBALION, accompanied by explanations and illustrations which we deem likely to render the teachings more easily comprehended by the modern student, particularly as the original text is purposely veiled in obscure terms.

The original maxims, axioms, and precepts of THE KYBALION are printed herein, in italics, the proper credit being given. Our own work is printed in the regular way, in the body of the work. We trust that the many students to whom we now offer this little work will derive as much benefit from the study of its pages as have the many who have gone on before, treading the same Path to Mastery throughout the centuries that have passed since the times of HERMES TRISMEGISTUS--the Master of Masters--the Great-Great. In the words of "THE KYBALION":

"Where fall the footsteps of the Master, the ears of those ready for his Teaching open wide."--The Kybalion.

"When the ears of the student are ready to hear, then cometh the lips to fill them with Wisdom."--The Kybalion.

So that according to the Teachings, the passage of this book to those ready for the instruction will attract the attention of such as are prepared to receive the Teaching. And, likewise, when the pupil is ready to receive the truth, then will this little book come to him, or her. Such is The Law. The Hermetic Principle of Cause and Effect, in its aspect of The Law of Attraction, will bring lips and ear together--pupil and book in company. So mote it be!

CHAPTER II

THE SEVEN HERMETIC PRINCIPLES

"The Principles of Truth are Seven; he who knows these, understandingly, possesses the Magic Key before whose touch all the Doors of the Temple fly open."--The Kybalion.

The Seven Hermetic Principles, upon which the entire Hermetic Philosophy is based, are as follows:

1. The Principle of Mentalism.
2. The Principle of Correspondence.
3. The Principle of Vibration.
4. The Principle of Polarity.
5. The Principle of Rhythm.
6. The Principle of Cause and Effect.
7. The Principle of Gender.

These Seven Principles will be discussed and explained as we proceed with these lessons. A short explanation of each, however, may as well be given at this point.

Seven Hermetic Principles

1. The Principle of Mentalism

"THE ALL IS MIND; The Universe is Mental."--The Kybalion.

This Principle embodies the truth that "All is Mind." It explains that THE ALL (which is the Substantial Reality underlying all the outward manifestations and appearances which we know under the terms of "The Material Universe"; the "Phenomena of Life"; "Matter"; "Energy"; and, in short, all that is apparent to our material senses) is SPIRIT which in itself is UNKNOWABLE and UNDEFINABLE, but which may be considered and thought of as AN UNIVERSAL, INFINITE, LIVING MIND. It also explains that all the phenomenal world or universe is simply a Mental Creation of THE ALL, subject to the Laws of Created Things, and that the universe, as a whole, and in its parts or units, has its existence in the Mind of THE ALL, in which Mind we "live and move and have our being." This Principle, by establishing the Mental Nature of the Universe, easily explains all of the varied mental and psychic phenomena that occupy such a large portion of the public attention, and which, without such explanation, are non-understandable and defy scientific treatment. An understanding of this great Hermetic Principle of Mentalism enables the individual to readily grasp the laws of the Mental Universe, and to apply the same to his well-being and advancement. The Hermetic Student is enabled to apply intelligently the great Mental Laws, instead of using them in a haphazard manner. With the Master-Key in his possession, the student may unlock the many doors of the mental and psychic temple of knowledge, and enter the same freely and intelligently. This Principle explains the true nature of "Energy," "Power," and "Matter," and why and how all these are subordinate to the Mastery of Mind. One of the old Hermetic Masters wrote, long ages ago: "He who grasps the truth of the Mental Nature of the Universe is well advanced on The Path to Mastery." And these words are as true today as at the time they

The Kybalion

were first written. Without this Master-Key, Mastery is impossible, and the student knocks in vain at the many doors of The Temple.

Seven Hermetic Principles

2. The Principle of Correspondence

"As above, so below; as below, so above."
--The Kybalion.

This Principle embodies the truth that there is always a Correspondence between the laws and phenomena of the various planes of Being and Life. The old Hermetic axiom ran in these words: "As above, so below; as below, so above." And the grasping of this Principle gives one the means of solving many a dark paradox, and hidden secret of Nature. There are planes beyond our knowing, but when we apply the Principle of Correspondence to them we are able to understand much that would otherwise be unknowable to us. This Principle is of universal application and manifestation, on the various planes of the material, mental, and spiritual universe--it is an Universal Law. The ancient Hermetists considered this Principle as one of the most important mental instruments by which man was able to pry aside the obstacles which hid from view the Unknown. Its use even tore aside the Veil of Isis to the extent that a glimpse of the face of the goddess might be caught. Just as a knowledge of the Principles of Geometry enables man to measure distant suns and their movements, while seated in his observatory, so a knowledge of the Principle of Correspondence enables Man to reason intelligently from the Known to the Unknown. Studying the monad, he understands the archangel.

3. The Principle of Vibration

"Nothing rests; everything moves; everything vibrates." — The Kybalion.

This Principle embodies the truth that "everything is in motion"; "everything vibrates"; "nothing is at rest"; facts which Modern Science endorses, and which each new scientific discovery tends to verify. And yet this Hermetic Principle was enunciated thousands of years ago, by the Masters of Ancient Egypt. This Principle explains that the differences between different manifestations of Matter, Energy, Mind, and even Spirit, result largely from varying rates of Vibration. From THE ALL, which is Pure Spirit, down to the grossest form of Matter, all is in vibration--the higher the vibration, the higher the position in the scale. The vibration of Spirit is at such an infinite rate of intensity and rapidity that it is practically at rest--just as a rapidly moving wheel seems to be motionless. And at the other end of the scale, there are gross forms of matter whose vibrations are so low as to seem at rest. Between these poles, there are millions upon millions of varying degrees of vibration. From corpuscle and electron, atom and molecule, to worlds and universes, everything is in vibratory motion. This is also true on the planes of energy and force (which are but varying degrees of vibration); and also on the mental planes (whose states depend upon vibrations); and even on to the spiritual planes. An understanding of this Principle, with the appropriate formulas, enables Hermetic students to control their own mental vibrations as well as those of others. The Masters also apply this Principle to the conquering of Natural phenomena, in various ways. "He who understands the Principle of Vibration, has grasped the scepter of power," says one of the old writers.

Seven Hermetic Principles

4. The Principle of Polarity

"Everything is Dual; everything has poles; everything has its pair of opposites; like and unlike are the same; opposites are identical in nature, but different in degree; extremes meet; all truths are but half-truths; all paradoxes may be reconciled."--The Kybalion.

This Principle embodies the truth that "everything is dual"; "everything has two poles"; "everything has its pair of opposites," all of which were old Hermetic axioms. It explains the old paradoxes, that have perplexed so many, which have been stated as follows: "Thesis and antithesis are identical in nature, but different in degree"; "opposites are the same, differing only in degree"; "the pairs of opposites may be reconciled"; "extremes meet"; "everything is and isn't, at the same time"; "all truths are but half-truths"; "every truth is half-false"; "there are two sides to everything," etc., etc., etc. It explains that in everything there are two poles, or opposite aspects, and that "opposites" are really only the two extremes of the same thing, with many varying degrees between them. To illustrate: Heat and Cold, although "opposites," are really the same thing, the differences consisting merely of degrees of the same thing. Look at your thermometer and see if you can discover where "heat" terminates and "cold" begins! There is no such thing as "absolute heat" or "absolute cold"--the two terms "heat" and "cold" simply indicate varying degrees of the same thing, and that "same thing" which manifests as "heat" and "cold" is merely a form, variety, and rate of Vibration. So "heat" and "cold" are simply the "two poles" of that which we call "Heat"--and the phenomena attendant thereupon are manifestations of the Principle of Polarity. The same Principle manifests in the case of "Light and Darkness," which are the same thing, the difference consisting of varying degrees between the two poles of the phenomena. Where does "darkness" leave off, and "light" begin? What is the difference between "Large and Small"? Between "Hard and Soft"? Between "Black and White"? Between "Sharp and Dull"? Between "Noise and Quiet"? Between "High and Low"? Between "Positive and Negative"? The Principle of Polarity explains these paradoxes, and no other Principle can supersede it. The same Principle operates on the Mental Plane. Let us take a radical and extreme example--that of "Love and Hate," two mental states apparently totally different. And yet there are degrees of Hate and degrees of Love, and a middle point in which we use the terms "Like or Dislike," which shade into each other so gradually that sometimes we are at a loss to know whether we "like" or "dislike" or "neither." And all are simply degrees of the same thing, as you will see if you will but think a moment. And, more than this (and considered of more importance by the Hermetists), it is possible to change the vibrations of Hate to the vibrations of Love, in one's own mind, and in the minds of others. Many of you, who read these lines, have had personal experiences of the involuntary rapid transition from Love to Hate, and the reverse, in your own case and that of others. And you will therefore realize the possibility of this being accomplished by the use of the Will, by means of the Hermetic formulas. "Good and Evil" are but the poles of the same thing, and the Hermetist understands the art of transmuting Evil into Good, by means of an application of the Principle of Polarity. In short, the "Art of Polarization" becomes a phase of "Mental Alchemy" known and practiced by the ancient and modern Hermetic Masters. An understanding of the Principle will enable one to change his own Polarity, as well as that of others, if he will devote the time and study necessary to master the art.

5. The Principle of Rhythm

"Everything flows, out and in; everything has its tides; all things rise and fall; the pendulum-swing manifests in everything; the measure of the swing to the right is the measure of the swing to the left; rhythm compensates." — The Kybalion.

This Principle embodies the truth that in everything there is manifested a measured motion, to and fro; a flow and inflow; a swing backward and forward; a pendulum-like movement; a tide-like ebb and flow; a high-tide and low-tide; between the two poles which exist in accordance with the Principle of Polarity described a moment ago. There is always an action and a reaction; an advance and a retreat; a rising and a sinking. This is in the affairs of the Universe, suns, worlds, men, animals, mind, energy, and matter. This law is manifest in the creation and destruction of worlds; in the rise and fall of nations; in the life of all things; and finally in the mental states of Man (and it is with this latter that the Hermetists find the understanding of the Principle most important). The Hermetists have grasped this Principle, finding its universal application, and have also discovered certain means to overcome its effects in themselves by the use of the appropriate formulas and methods. They apply the Mental Law of Neutralization. They cannot annul the Principle, or cause it to cease its operation, but they have learned how to escape its effects upon themselves to a certain degree depending upon the Mastery of the Principle. They have learned how to USE it, instead of being USED BY it. In this and similar methods, consist the Art of the Hermetists. The Master of Hermetics polarizes himself at the point at which he desires to rest, and then neutralizes the Rhythmic swing of the pendulum which would tend to carry him to the other pole. All individuals who have attained any degree of Self-Mastery do this to a certain degree, more or less unconsciously, but the Master does this consciously, and by the use of his Will, and attains a degree of Poise and Mental Firmness almost impossible of belief on the part of the masses who are swung backward and forward like a pendulum. This Principle and that of Polarity have been closely studied by the Hermetists, and the methods of counteracting, neutralizing, and USING them form an important part of the Hermetic Mental Alchemy.

Seven Hermetic Principles

6. The Principle of Cause and Effect

"Every Cause has its Effect; every Effect has its Cause; everything happens according to Law; Chance is but a name for Law not recognized; there are many planes of causation, but nothing escapes the Law."--The Kybalion.

This Principle embodies the fact that there is a Cause for every Effect; an Effect from every Cause. It explains that: "Everything Happens according to Law"; that nothing ever "merely happens"; that there is no such thing as Chance; that while there are various planes of Cause and Effect, the higher dominating the lower planes, still nothing ever entirely escapes the Law. The Hermetists understand the art and methods of rising above the ordinary plane of Cause and Effect, to a certain degree, and by mentally rising to a higher plane they become Causers instead of Effects. The masses of people are carried along, obedient to environment; the wills and desires of others stronger than themselves; heredity; suggestion; and other outward causes moving them about like pawns on the Chessboard of Life. But the Masters, rising to the plane above, dominate their moods, characters, qualities, and powers, as well as the environment surrounding them, and become Movers instead of pawns. They help to PLAY THE GAME OF LIFE, instead of being played and moved about by other wills and environment. They USE the Principle instead of being its tools. The Masters obey the Causation of the higher planes, but they help to RULE on their own plane. In this statement there is condensed a wealth of Hermetic knowledge--let him read who can.

7. The Principle of Gender

"Gender is in everything; everything has its Masculine and Feminine Principles; Gender manifests on all planes."--The Kybalion.

This Principle embodies the truth that there is GENDER manifested in everything--the Masculine and Feminine Principles ever at work. This is true not only of the Physical Plane, but of the Mental and even the Spiritual Planes. On the Physical Plane, the Principle manifests as SEX, on the higher planes it takes higher forms, but the Principle is ever the same. No creation, physical, mental or spiritual, is possible without this Principle. An understanding of its laws will throw light on many a subject that has perplexed the minds of men. The Principle of Gender works ever in the direction of generation, regeneration, and creation. Everything, and every person, contains the two Elements or Principles, or this great Principle, within it, him or her. Every Male thing has the Female Element also; every Female contains also the Male Principle. If you would understand the philosophy of Mental and Spiritual Creation, Generation, and Re-generation, you must understand and study this Hermetic Principle. It contains the solution of many mysteries of Life. We caution you that this Principle has no reference to the many base, pernicious and degrading lustful theories, teachings and practices, which are taught under fanciful titles, and which are a prostitution of the great natural principle of Gender. Such base revivals of the ancient infamous forms of Phallicism tend to ruin mind, body and soul, and the Hermetic Philosophy has ever sounded the warning note against these degraded teachings which tend toward lust, licentiousness, and perversion of Nature's principles. If you seek such teachings, you must go elsewhere for them--Hermeticism contains nothing for you along these lines. To the pure, all things are pure; to the base, all things are base.

CHAPTER III

MENTAL TRANSMUTATION

"Mind (as well as metals and elements) may be transmuted, from state to state; degree to degree; condition to condition; pole to pole; vibration to vibration. True Hermetic Transmutation is a Mental Art."--The Kybalion.

As we have stated, the Hermetists were the original alchemists, astrologers, and psychologists, Hermes having been the founder of these schools of thought. From astrology has grown modern astronomy; from alchemy has grown modern chemistry; from the mystic psychology has grown the modern psychology of the schools. But it must not be supposed that the ancients were ignorant of that which the modern schools suppose to be their exclusive and special property. The records engraved on the stones of Ancient Egypt show conclusively that the ancients had a full comprehensive knowledge of astronomy, the very building of the Pyramids showing the connection between their design and the study of astronomical science. Nor were they ignorant of Chemistry, for the fragments of the ancient writings show that they were acquainted with the chemical properties of things; in fact, the ancient theories regarding physics are being slowly verified by the latest discoveries of modern science, notably those relating to the constitution of matter. Nor must it be supposed that they were ignorant of the so-called modern discoveries in psychology--on the contrary, the Egyptians were especially skilled in the science of Psychology, particularly in the branches that the modern schools ignore, but which, nevertheless, are being uncovered under the name of "psychic science" which is perplexing the psychologists of to-day, and making them reluctantly admit that "there may be something in it after all."

The Kybalion

The truth is, that beneath the material chemistry, astronomy and psychology (that is, the psychology in its phase of "brain-action") the ancients possessed a knowledge of transcendental astronomy, called astrology; of transcendental chemistry, called alchemy; of transcendental psychology, called mystic psychology. They possessed the Inner Knowledge as well as the Outer Knowledge, the latter alone being possessed by modern scientists. Among the many secret branches of knowledge possessed by the Hermetists, was that known as Mental Transmutation, which forms the subject matter of this lesson.

"Transmutation" is a term usually employed to designate the ancient art of the transmutation of metals--particularly of the base metals into gold. The word "Transmute" means "to change from one nature, form, or substance, into another; to transform" (Webster). And accordingly, "Mental Transmutation" means the art of changing and transforming mental states, forms, and conditions, into others. So you may see that Mental Transmutation is the "Art of Mental Chemistry," if you like the term--a form of practical Mystic Psychology.

But this means far more than appears on the surface. Transmutation, Alchemy, or Chemistry on the Mental Plane is important enough in its effects, to be sure, and if the art stopped there it would still be one of the most important branches of study known to man. But this is only the beginning. Let us see why!

The first of the Seven Hermetic Principles is the Principle of Mentalism, the axiom of which is "THE ALL is Mind; the Universe is Mental," which means that the Underlying Reality of the Universe is Mind; and the Universe itself is Mental--that is, "existing in the Mind of THE ALL." We shall consider this Principle in succeeding lessons, but let us see the effect of the principle if it be assumed to be true.

Mental Transmutation

If the Universe is Mental in its nature, then Mental Transmutation must be the art of CHANGING THE CONDITIONS OF THE UNIVERSE, along the lines of Matter, Force and mind. So you see, therefore, that Mental Transmutation is really the "Magic" of which the ancient; writers had so much to say in their mystical works, and about which they gave so few practical instructions. If All be Mental, then the art which enables one to transmute mental conditions must render the Master the controller of material conditions as well as those ordinarily called "mental."

As a matter of fact, none but advanced Mental Alchemists have been able to attain the degree of power necessary to control the grosser physical conditions, such as the control of the elements of Nature; the production or cessation of tempests; the production and cessation of earthquakes and other great physical phenomena. But that such men have existed, and do exist today, is a matter of earnest belief to all advanced occultists of all schools. That the Masters exist, and have these powers, the best teachers assure their students, having had experiences which justify them in such belief and statements. These Masters do not make public exhibitions of their powers, but seek seclusion from the crowds of men, in order to better work their may along the Path of Attainment. We mention their existence, at this point, merely to call your attention to the fact that their power is entirely Mental, and operates along the lines of the higher Mental Transmutation, under the Hermetic Principle of Mentalism.

"The Universe is Mental"--The Kybalion.

But students and Hermetists of lesser degree than Masters--the Initiates and Teachers--are able to freely work along the Mental Plane, in Mental Transmutation. In fact all that we call "psychic phenomena,"; "mental influence"; "mental science"; "new-thought phenomena," etc., operates along the same general lines, for there is but one principle involved, no matter by what name the phenomena be called.

The student and practitioner of Mental Transmutation works among the Mental Plane, transmuting mental conditions, states, etc., into others, according to various formulas, more or less efficacious. The various "treatments," "affirmations," "denials" etc., of the schools of mental science are but formulas, often quite imperfect and unscientific, of The Hermetic Art. The majority of modern practitioners are quite ignorant compared to the ancient masters, for they lack the fundamental knowledge upon which the work is based.

Not only may the mental states, etc., of one's self be changed or transmuted by Hermetic Methods; but also the states of others may be, and are, constantly transmuted in the same way, usually unconsciously, but often consciously by some understanding the laws and principles, in cases where the people affected are not informed of the principles of self-protection. And more than this, as many students and practitioners of modern mental science know, every material condition depending upon the minds of other people may be changed or transmuted in accordance with the earnest desire, will, and "treatments" of person desiring changed conditions of life. The public are so generally informed regarding these things at present, that we do not deem it necessary to mention the same at length, our purpose at this point being merely to show the Hermetic Principle and Art underlying all of these various forms of practice, good and evil, for the force can be used in opposite directions according to the Hermetic Principles of Polarity.

In this little book we shall state the basic principles of Mental Transmutation, that all who read may grasp the Underlying Principles, and thus possess the Master-Key that will unlock the many doors of the Principle of Polarity.

Mental Transmutation

We shall now proceed to a consideration of the first of the Hermetic Seven Principles--the Principle of Mentalism, in which is explained the truth that "THE ALL is Mind; the Universe is Mental," in the words of The Kybalion. We ask the close attention, and careful study of this great Principle, on the part of our students, for it is really the Basic Principle of the whole Hermetic Philosophy, and of the Hermetic Art of Mental Transmutation.

CHAPTER IV

THE ALL

"Under, and back of, the Universe of Time, Space and Change, is ever to be found The Substantial Reality--the Fundamental Truth."--The Kybalion.

"Substance" means: "that which underlies all outward manifestations; the essence; the essential reality; the thing in itself," etc. "Substantial" means: "actually existing; being the essential element; being real," etc. "Reality" means: "the state of being real; true, enduring; valid; fixed; permanent; actual," etc.

Under and behind all outward appearances or manifestations, there must always be a Substantial Reality. This is the Law. Man considering the Universe, of which he is a unit, sees nothing but change in matter, forces, and mental states. He sees that nothing really IS, but that everything is BECOMING and CHANGING. Nothing stands still-everything is being born, growing, dying-the very instant a thing reaches its height, it begins to decline--the law of rhythm is in constant operation--there is no reality, enduring quality, fixity, or substantiality in anything-- nothing is permanent but Change. He sees all things evolving from other things, and resolving into other things--constant action and reaction; inflow and outflow; building up and tearing down; creation and destruction; birth, growth and death. Nothing endures but Change. And if he be a thinking man, he realizes that all of these changing things must be but outward appearances or manifestations of some Underlying Power--some Substantial Reality.

All thinkers, in all lands and in all times, have assumed the necessity for postulating the existence of this Substantial Reality. All philosophies worthy of the name have been based upon this

The All

thought. Men have given to this Substantial Reality many names--some have called it by the term of Deity (under many titles). Others have called it "The Infinite and Eternal Energy" others have tried to call it "Matter"--but all have acknowledged its existence. It is self-evident it needs no argument.

In these lessons we have followed the example of some of the world's greatest thinkers, both ancient and modern--the Hermetic. Masters--and have called this Underlying Power--this Substantial Reality--by the Hermetic name of "THE ALL," which term we consider the most comprehensive of the many terms applied by Man to THAT which transcends names and terms.

We accept and teach the view of the great Hermetic thinkers of all times, as well as of those illumined souls who have reached higher planes of being, both of whom assert that the inner nature of THE ALL is UNKNOWABLE. This must be so, for naught by THE ALL itself can comprehend its own nature and being.

The Hermetists believe and teach that THE ALL, "in itself," is and must ever be UNKNOWABLE. They regard all the theories, guesses and speculations of the theologians and metaphysicians regarding the inner nature of THE ALL, as but the childish efforts of mortal minds to grasp the secret of the Infinite. Such efforts have always failed and will always fail, from the very nature of the task. One pursuing such inquiries travels around and around in the labyrinth of thought, until he is lost to all sane reasoning, action or conduct, and is utterly unfitted for the work of life. He is like the squirrel which frantically runs around and around the circling treadmill wheel of his cage, traveling ever and yet reaching nowhere--at the end a prisoner still, and standing just where he started.

And still more presumptuous are those who attempt to ascribe to THE ALL the personality, qualities, properties, characteristics and attributes of themselves, ascribing to THE ALL the human emotions, feelings, and characteristics, even down to the pettiest qualities of mankind, such as jealousy, susceptibility to flattery and praise, desire for offerings and worship, and all the other survivals from the days of the childhood of the race. Such ideas are not worthy of grown men and women, and are rapidly being discarded.

(At this point, it may be proper for me to state that we make a distinction between Religion and Theology--between Philosophy and Metaphysics. Religion, to us, means that intuitional realization of the existence of THE ALL, and one's relationship to it; while Theology means the attempts of men to ascribe personality, qualities, and characteristics to it; their theories regarding its affairs, will, desires, plans, and designs, and their assumption of the office of " middle-men" between THE ALL and the people. Philosophy, to us, means the inquiry after knowledge of things knowable and thinkable; while Metaphysics means the attempt to carry the inquiry over and beyond the boundaries and into regions unknowable and unthinkable, and with the same tendency as that of Theology. And consequently, both Religion and Philosophy mean to us things having roots in Reality, while Theology and Metaphysics seem like broken reeds, rooted in the quicksands of ignorance, and affording naught but the most insecure support for the mind or soul of Man. we do not insist upon our students accepting these definitions--we mention them merely to show our position. At any rate, you shall hear very little about Theology and Metaphysics in these lessons.)

But while the essential nature of THE ALL is Unknowable, there are certain truths connected with its existence which the human mind finds itself compelled to accept. And an examination of these reports form a proper subject of inquiry, particularly as they agree

The All

with the reports of the Illumined on higher planes. And to this inquiry we now invite you.

"THAT which is the Fundamental Truth--the Substantial Reality--is beyond true naming, but the Wise Men call it THE ALL."--The Kybalion.

"In its Essence, THE ALL is UNKNOWABLE."--The Kybalion.

"But, the report of Reason must be hospitably received, and treated with respect."--The Kybalion.

The human reason, whose reports we must accept so long as we think at all, informs us as follows regarding THE ALL, and that without attempting to remove the veil of the Unknowable:

(1) THE ALL must be ALL that REALLY IS. There can be nothing existing outside of THE ALL, else THE ALL would not be THE ALL.

(2) THE ALL must be INFINITE, for there is nothing else to define, confine, bound, limit; or restrict THE ALL. It must be Infinite in Time, or ETERNAL,--it must have always continuously existed, for there is nothing else to have ever created it, and something can never evolve from nothing, and if it had ever "not been," even for a moment, it would not "be" now,--it must continuously exist forever, for there is nothing to destroy it, and it can never "not-be," even for a moment, because something can never become nothing. It must be Infinite in Space--it must be Everywhere, for there is no place outside of THE ALL—it cannot be otherwise than continuous in Space, without break, cessation, separation, or interruption, for there is nothing to break, separate, or interrupt its continuity, and nothing with which to "fill in the gaps." It must be Infinite in Power, or Absolute, for there is nothing to limit, restrict, restrain, confine, disturb or condition it--it is subject to no other Power, for there is no other Power.

(3) THE ALL must be IMMUTABLE, or not subject to change in its real nature, for there is nothing to work changes upon it nothing into which it could change, nor from which it could have changed. It cannot be added to nor subtracted from; increased nor diminished; nor become greater or lesser in any respect whatsoever. It must have always been, and must always remain, just what it is now--THE ALL--there has never been, is not now, and never will be, anything else into which it can change.

THE ALL being Infinite, Absolute, Eternal and Unchangeable it must follow that anything finite, changeable, fleeting, and conditioned cannot be THE ALL. And as there is Nothing outside of THE ALL, in Reality, then any and all such finite things must be as Nothing in Reality. Now do not become befogged, nor frightened--we are not trying to lead you into the Christian Science field under cover of Hermetic Philosophy. There is a Reconciliation of this apparently contradictory state of affairs. Be patient, we will reach it in time.

We see around us that which is called "Matter," which forms the physical foundation for all forms. Is THE ALL merely Matter? Not at all! Matter cannot manifest Life or Mind, and as Life and Mind are manifested in the Universe, THE ALL cannot be Matter, for nothing rises higher than its own source--nothing is ever manifested in an effect that is not in the cause--nothing is evolved as a consequent that is not involved as an antecedent. And then Modern Science informs us that there is really no such thing as Matter--that what we call Matter is merely "interrupted energy or force," that is, energy or force at a low rate of vibration. As a recent writer has said "Matter has melted into Mystery." Even Material Science has abandoned the theory of Matter, and now rests on the basis of "Energy."

Then is THE ALL mere Energy or Force? Not Energy or Force as the materialists use the terms, for their energy and force are blind,

The All

mechanical things, devoid of Life or Mind. Life and Mind can never evolve from blind Energy or Force, for the reason given a moment ago: "Nothing can rise higher than its source--nothing is evolved unless it is involved--nothing manifests in the effect, unless it is in the cause. " And so THE ALL cannot be mere Energy or Force, for, if it were, then there would be no such things as Life and Mind in existence, and we know better than that, for we are Alive and using Mind to consider this very question, and so are those who claim that Energy or Force is Everything.

What is there then higher than Matter or Energy that we know to be existent in the Universe? LIFE AND MIND! Life and Mind in all their varying degrees of unfoldment! "Then," you ask, "do you mean to tell us that THE ALL is LIFE and MIND?" Yes! and No! is our answer. If you mean Life and Mind as we poor petty mortals know them, we say No! THE ALL is not that! "But what kind of Life and Mind do you mean?" you ask.

The answer is "LIVING MIND," as far above that which mortals know by those words, as Life and Mind are higher than mechanical forces, or matter--INFINITE LIVING MIND as compared to finite "Life and Mind." We mean that which the illumined souls mean when they reverently pronounce the word: "SPIRIT!"

"THE ALL" is Infinite Living Mind--the Illumined call it SPIRIT!

CHAPTER V

THE MENTAL UNIVERSE

"The Universe is Mental--held in the Mind of THE ALL."--The Kybalion.

THE ALL is SPIRIT! But what is Spirit? This question cannot be answered, for the reason that its definition is practically that of THE ALL, which cannot be explained or defined. Spirit is simply a name that men give to the highest conception of Infinite Living Mind--it means "the Real Essence"--it means Living Mind, as much superior to Life and Mind as we know them, as the latter are superior to mechanical Energy and Matter. Spirit transcends our understanding, and we use the term merely that we may think or speak of THE ALL. For the purposes of thought and understanding, we are justified in thinking of Spirit as Infinite Living Mind, at the same time acknowledging that we cannot fully understand it. We must either do this or stop thinking of the matter at all.

Let us now proceed to a consideration of the nature of the Universe, as a whole and in its parts. What is the Universe? We have seen that there can be nothing outside of THE ALL. Then is the Universe THE ALL? No, this cannot be, because the Universe seems to be made up of MANY, and is constantly changing, and in other ways it does not measure up to the ideas that we are compelled to accept regarding THE ALL, as stated in our last lesson. Then if the Universe be not THE ALL, then it must be Nothing--such is the inevitable conclusion of the mind at first thought. But this will not satisfy the question, for we are sensible of the existence of the Universe. Then if the Universe is neither THE ALL, nor Nothing, what Can it be? Let us examine this question.

The Mental Universe

If the Universe exists at all, or seems to exist, it must proceed in some way from THE ALL--it must be a creation of THE ALL. But as something can never come from nothing, from what could THE ALL have created it. Some philosophers have answered this question by saying that THE ALL created the Universe from ITSELF--that is, from the being and substance of THE ALL. But this will not do, for THE ALL cannot be subtracted from, nor divided, as we have seen, and then again if this be so, would not each particle in the Universe be aware of its being THE ALL--THE ALL could not lose its knowledge of itself, nor actually BECOME an atom, or blind force, or lowly living thing. Some men, indeed, realizing that THE ALL is indeed ALL, and also recognizing that they, the men, existed, have jumped to the conclusion that they and THE ALL were identical, and they have filled the air with shouts of "I AM GOD," to the amusement of the multitude and the sorrow of sages. The claim of the corpuscle that: "I am Man!" would be modest in comparison.

But, what indeed is the Universe, if it be not THE ALL, not yet created by THE ALL having separated itself into fragments? What else can it be-- of what else can it be made? This is the great question. Let us examine it carefully. We find here that the "Principle of Correspondence" (see Lesson I.) comes to our aid here. The old Hermetic axiom, "As above so below," may be pressed into service at this point. Let us endeavor to get a glimpse of the workings on higher planes by examining those on our own. The Principle of Correspondence must apply to this as well as to other problems.

Let us see! On his own plane of being, how does Man create? Well, first, he may create by making something out of outside materials. But this will not do, for there are no materials outside of THE ALL with which it may create. Well, then, secondly, Man pro-creates or reproduces his kind by the process of begetting, which is self-multiplication accomplished by transferring a portion of his substance to his offspring. But this will not do, because THE ALL cannot transfer or subtract a portion of itself, nor can it reproduce or multiply itself--in the first place there would be a taking away, and in the second case a multiplication or addition to THE ALL, both thoughts being an absurdity. Is there no third way in which MAN creates? Yes, there is--he CREATES MENTALLY! And in so doing he uses no outside materials, nor does he reproduce himself, and yet his Spirit pervades the Mental Creation.

Following the Principle of Correspondence, we are justified in considering that THE ALL creates the Universe MENTALLY, in a manner akin to the process whereby Man creates Mental Images. And, here is where the report of Reason tallies precisely with the report of the Illumined, as shown by their teachings and writings. Such are the teachings of the Wise Men. Such was the Teaching of Hermes.

THE ALL can create in no other way except mentally, without either using material (and there is none to use), or else reproducing itself (which is also impossible). There is no escape from this conclusion of the Reason, which, as we have said, agrees with the highest teachings of the Illumined. Just as you, student, may create a Universe of your own in your mentality, so does THE ALL create Universes in its own Mentality. But your Universe is the mental creation of a Finite Mind, whereas that of THE ALL is the creation of an Infinite. The two are similar in kind, but infinitely different in degree. We shall examine more closely into the process of creation and manifestation as we proceed. But this is the point to fix in your minds at this stage: THE UNIVERSE, AND ALL IT CONTAINS, IS A MENTAL CREATION OF THE ALL. Verily indeed, ALL IS MIND!

"THE ALL creates in its Infinite Mind countless Universes, which exist for aeons of Time--and yet, to THE ALL, the creation,

The Mental Universe

development, decline and death of a million Universes is as the time of the twinkling of an eye."--The Kybalion.

"The Infinite Mind of THE ALL is the womb of Universes." — The Kybalion.

The Principle of Gender (see Lesson I. and other lessons to follow) is manifested on all planes of life, material mental and spiritual. But, as we have said before, "Gender" does not mean "Sex" sex is merely a material manifestation of gender. "Gender" means "relating to generation or creation." And whenever anything is generated or created, on any plane, the Principle of Gender must be manifested. And this is true even in the creation of Universes.

Now do not jump to the conclusion that we are teaching that there is a male and female God, or Creator. That idea is merely a distortion of the ancient teachings on the subject. The true teaching is that THE ALL, in itself, is above Gender, as it is above every other Law, including those of Time and Space. It is the Law, from which the Laws proceed, and it is not subject to them. But when THE ALL manifests on the plane of generation or creation, then it acts according to Law and Principle, for it is moving on a lower plane of Being. And consequently it manifests the Principle of Gender, in its Masculine and Feminine aspects, on the Mental Plane, of course.

This idea may seem startling to some of you who hear it for the first time, but you have all really passively accepted it in your everyday conceptions. You speak of the Fatherhood of God, and the Motherhood of Nature--of God, the Divine Father, and Nature the Universal Mother--and have thus instinctively acknowledged the Principle of Gender in the Universe. Is this not so?

But, the Hermetic teaching does not imply a real duality--THE ALL is ONE--the Two Aspects are merely aspects of manifestation. The teaching is that The Masculine Principle manifested by THE

ALL stands, in a way, apart from the actual mental creation of the Universe. It projects its Will toward the Feminine Principle (which may be called "Nature") whereupon the latter begins the actual work of the evolution of the Universe, from simple "centers of activity" on to man, and then on and on still higher, all according to well-established and firmly enforced Laws of Nature. If you prefer the old figures of thought, you may think of the Masculine Principle as GOD, the Father, and of the Feminine Principle as NATURE, the Universal Mother, from whose womb all things have been born. This is more than a mere poetic figure of speech-- it is an idea of the actual process of the creation of the Universe. But always remember, that THE ALL is but One, and that in its Infinite Mind the Universe is generated, created and exists.

It may help you to get the proper idea, if you will apply the Law of Correspondence to yourself, and your own mind. You know that the part of You which you call "I," in a sense, stands apart and witnesses the creation of mental Images in your own mind. The part of your mind in which the mental generation is accomplished may be called the "Me" in distinction from the "I" which stands apart and witnesses and examines the thoughts, ideas and images of the "Me." "As above, so below," remember, and the phenomena of one plane may be employed to solve the riddles of higher or lower planes.

Is it any wonder that You, the child, feel that instinctive reverence for THE ALL, which feeling we call "religion"--that respect, and reverence for THE FATHER MIND? Is it any wonder that, when you consider the works and wonders of Nature, you are overcome with a mighty feeling which has its roots away down in your inmost being? It is the MOTHER MIND that you are pressing close up to, like a babe to the breast.

Do not make the mistake of supposing that the little world you see around you--the Earth, which is a mere grain of dust in the

The Mental Universe

Universe--is the Universe itself. There are millions upon millions of such worlds, and greater. And there are millions of millions of such Universes in existence within the Infinite Mind of THE ALL. And even in our own little solar system there are regions and planes of life far higher than ours, and beings compared to which we earth-bound mortals are as the slimy life-forms that dwell on the ocean's bed when compared to Man. There are beings with powers and attributes higher than Man has ever dreamed of the gods' possessing. And yet these beings were once as you, and still lower--and you will be even as they, and still higher, in time, for such is the Destiny of Man as reported by the Illumined.

And Death is not real, even in the Relative sense--it is but Birth to a new life--and You shall go on, and on, and on, to higher and still higher planes of life, for aeons upon aeons of time. The Universe is your home, and you shall explore its farthest recesses before the end of Time. You are dwelling in the Infinite Mind of THE ALL, and your possibilities and opportunities are infinite, both in time and space. And at the end of the Grand Cycle of Aeons, when THE ALL shall draw back into itself all of its creations--you will go gladly for you will then be able to know the Whole Truth of being At One with THE ALL. Such is the report of the Illumined--those who have advanced well along The Path.

And, in the meantime, rest calm and serene--you are safe and protected by the Infinite Power of the FATHER-MOTHER MIND.

"Within the Father-Mother Mind, mortal children are at home."--The Kybalion.

"There is not one who is Fatherless, nor Motherless in the Universe."--The Kybalion.

CHAPTER VI

THE DIVINE PARADOX

"The half-wise, recognizing the comparative unreality of the Universe, imagine that they may defy its Laws—such are vain and presumptuous fools, and they are broken against the rocks and torn asunder by the elements by reason of their folly. The truly wise, knowing the nature of the Universe, use Law against laws; the higher against the lower; and by the Art of Alchemy transmute that which is undesirable into that which is worthy, and thus triumph. Mastery consists not in abnormal dreams, visions and fantastic imaginings or living, but in using the higher forces against the lower—escaping the pains of the lower planes by vibrating on the higher. Transmutation, not presumptuous denial, is the weapon of the Master."--The Kybalion.

This is the Paradox of the Universe, resulting from the Principle of Polarity which manifests when THE ALL begins to Create--hearken to it for it points the difference between half-wisdom and wisdom. While to THE INFINITE ALL, the Universe, its Laws, its Powers, its life, its Phenomena, are as things witnessed in the state of Meditation or Dream; yet to all that is Finite, the Universe must be treated as Real, and life, and action, and thought, must be based thereupon, accordingly, although with an ever understanding of the Higher Truth. Each according to its own Plane and Laws. Were THE ALL to imagine that the Universe were indeed Reality, then woe to the Universe, for there would be then no escape from lower to higher, divineward--then would the Universe become a fixity and progress would become impossible. And if Man, owing to half-wisdom, acts and lives and thinks of the Universe as merely a dream (akin to his own finite dreams) then indeed does it so become for him, and like a sleep-walker he stumbles ever around and around in a circle, making no progress, and being forced into

The Divine Paradox

an awakening at last by his falling bruised and bleeding over the Natural Laws which he ignored. Keep your mind ever on the Star, but let your eyes watch over your footsteps, lest you fall into the mire by reason of your upward gaze. Remember the Divine Paradox, that while the Universe IS NOT, still IT IS. Remember ever the Two Poles of Truth the Absolute and the Relative. Beware of Half-Truths.

What Hermetists know as "the Law of Paradox" is an aspect of the Principle of Polarity. The Hermetic writings are filled with references to the appearance of the Paradox in the consideration of the problems of Life and Being. The Teachers are constantly warning their students against the error of omitting the "other side" of any question. And their warnings are particularly directed to the problems of the Absolute and the Relative, which perplex all students of philosophy, and which cause so many to think and act contrary to what is generally known as "common sense." And we caution all students to be sure to grasp the Divine Paradox of the Absolute and Relative, lest they become entangled in the mire of the Half-Truth. With this in view this particular lesson has been written. Read it carefully!

The first thought that comes to the thinking man after he realizes the truth that the Universe is a Mental Creation of THE ALL, is that the Universe and all that it contains is a mere illusion; an unreality; against which idea his instincts revolt. But this, like all other great truths, must be considered both from the Absolute and the Relative points of view. From the Absolute viewpoint, of course, the Universe is in the nature of an illusion, a dream, a phantasmagoria, as compared to THE ALL in itself. We recognize this even in our ordinary view, for we speak of the world as "a fleeting show" that comes and goes, is born and dies--for the element of impermanence and change, finiteness and unsubstantiality, must ever be connected with the idea of a created

The Kybalion

Universe when it is contrasted with the idea of THE ALL, no matter what may be our beliefs concerning the nature of both. Philosopher, metaphysician, scientist and theologian all agree upon this idea, and the thought is found in all forms of philosophical thought and religious conceptions, as well as in the theories of the respective schools of metaphysics and theology.

So, the Hermetic Teachings do not preach the unsubstantiality of the Universe in any stronger terms than those more familiar to you, although their presentation of the subject may seem somewhat more startling. Anything that has a beginning and an ending must be, in a sense, unreal and untrue, and the Universe comes under the rule, in all schools of thought. From the Absolute point of view, there is nothing Real except THE ALL, no matter what terms we may use in thinking of, or discussing the subject. Whether the Universe be created of Matter, or whether it be a Mental Creation in the Mind of THE ALL--it is unsubstantial, non-enduring, a thing of time, space and change. We want you to realize this fact thoroughly, before you pass judgment on the Hermetic conception of the Mental nature of the Universe. Think over any and all of the other conceptions, and see whether this be not true of them.

But the Absolute point of view shows merely one side of the picture--the other side is the Relative one. Absolute Truth has been defined as "Things as the mind of God knows them," while Relative Truth is "Things as the highest reason of Man understands them." And so while to THE ALL the Universe must be unreal and illusionary, a mere dream or result of meditation,--nevertheless, to the finite minds forming a part of that Universe, and viewing it through mortal faculties, the Universe is very real indeed, and must be so considered. In recognizing the Absolute view, we must not make the mistake of ignoring or denying the facts and phenomena of the Universe as they present themselves to our mortal faculties--we are not THE ALL, remember.

The Divine Paradox

To take familiar illustrations, we all recognize the fact that matter "exists" to our senses--we will fare badly if we do not. And yet, even our finite minds understand the scientific dictum that there is no such thing as Matter from a scientific point of view--that which we call Matter is held to be merely an aggregation of atoms, which atoms themselves are merely a grouping of units of force, called electrons or "ions," vibrating and in constant circular motion. We kick a stone and we feel the impact--it seems to be real, notwithstanding that we know it to be merely what we have stated above. But remember that our foot, which feels the impact by means of our brains, is likewise Matter, so constituted of electrons, and for that matter so are our brains. And, at the best, if it were not by reason of our Mind, we would not know the foot or stone at all.

Then again, the ideal of the artist or sculptor, which he is endeavoring to reproduce in stone or on canvas, seems very real to him. So do the characters in the mind of the author; or dramatist, which he seeks to express so that others may recognize them. And if this be true in the case of our finite minds, what must be the degree of Reality in the Mental Images created in the Mind of the Infinite? Oh, friends, to mortals this Universe of Mentality is very real indeed--it is the only one we can ever know, though we rise from plane to plane, higher and higher in it. To know it otherwise, but actual experience, we must be THE ALL itself. It is true that the higher we rise in the scale--the nearer to "the mind of the Father" we reach--the more apparent becomes the illusory nature of finite things, but not until THE ALL finally withdraws us into itself does the vision actually vanish.

So, we need not dwell upon the feature of illusion. Rather let us, recognizing the real nature of the Universe, seek to understand its mental laws, and endeavor to use them to the best effect in our upward progress through life, as we travel from plane to plane of being. The Laws of the Universe are none the less "Iron Laws" because of the mental nature. All, except THE ALL, are bound by them. What is IN THE INFINITE MIND OF THE ALL is REAL in a degree second only to that Reality itself which is vested in the nature of THE ALL.

So, do not feel insecure or afraid--we are all HELD FIRMLY IN THE INFINITE MIND OF THE ALL, and there is naught to hurt us or for us to fear. There is no Power outside of THE ALL to affect us. So we may rest calm and secure. There is a world of comfort and security in this realization when once attained. Then "calm and peaceful do we sleep, rocked in the Cradle of the Deep"--resting safely on the bosom of the Ocean of Infinite Mind, which is THE ALL. In THE ALL, indeed, do "we live and move and have our being."

Matter is none the less Matter to us, while we dwell on the plane of Matter, although we know it to be merely an aggregation of "electrons," or particles of Force, vibrating rapidly and gyrating around each other in the formations of atoms; the atoms in turn vibrating and gyrating, forming molecules, which latter in turn form larger masses of Matter. Nor does Matter become less Matter, when we follow the inquiry still further, and learn from the Hermetic Teachings, that the "Force" of which the electrons are but units is merely a manifestation of the Mind of THE ALL, and like all else in the Universe is purely Mental in its nature. While on the Plane of matter, we must recognize its phenomena-- we may control Matter (as all Masters of higher or lesser degree do), but we do so by applying the higher forces. We commit a folly when we attempt to deny the existence of Matter in the relative aspect. We may deny its mastery over us--and rightly so--but we should not attempt to ignore it in its relative aspect, at least so long as we dwell upon its plane.

Nor do the Laws of Nature become less constant or effective, when we know them, likewise, to be merely mental creations. They are

The Divine Paradox

in full effect on the various planes. We overcome the lower laws, by applying still higher ones--and in this way only. But we cannot escape Law or rise above it entirely. Nothing but THE ALL can escape Law--and that because THE ALL is LAW itself, from which all Laws emerge. The most advanced Masters may acquire the powers usually attributed to the gods of men; and there are countless ranks of being, in the great hierarchy of life, whose being and power transcends even that of the highest Masters among men to a degree unthinkable by mortals, but even the highest Master, and the highest Being, must bow to the Law, and be as Nothing in the eye of THE ALL. So that if even these highest Beings, whose powers exceed even those attributed by men to their gods--if even these are bound by and are subservient to Law, then imagine the presumption of mortal man, of our race and grade, when he dares to consider the Laws of Nature as "unreal!" visionary and illusory, because he happens to be able to grasp the truth that the Laws are Mental in nature, and simply Mental Creations of THE ALL. Those Laws which THE ALL intends to be governing Laws are not to be defied or argued away. So long as the Universe endures, will they endure--for the Universe exists by virtue of these Laws which form its framework and which hold it together.

The Hermetic Principle of Mentalism, while explaining the true nature of the Universe upon the principle that all is Mental, does not change the scientific conceptions of the Universe, Life, or Evolution. In fact, science merely corroborates the Hermetic Teachings. The latter merely teaches that the nature of the Universe is "Mental," while modern science has taught that it is "Material"; or (of late) that it is "Energy" at the last analysis. The Hermetic Teachings have no fault to find with Herbert Spencer's basic principle which postulates the existence of an "Infinite and Eternal Energy, from which all things proceed." In fact, the Hermetics recognize in Spencer's philosophy the highest outside statement of the workings of the Natural Laws that have ever been

The Kybalion

promulgated, and they believe Spencer to have been a reincarnation of an ancient philosopher who dwelt in ancient Egypt thousands of years ago, and who later incarnated as Heraclitus, the Grecian philosopher who lived B. C. 500. And they regard his statement of the "Infinite and Eternal Energy" as directly in the line of the Hermetic Teachings, always with the addition of their own doctrine that his "Energy" is the Energy of the Mind of THE ALL. With the Master-Key of the Hermetic Philosophy, the student of Spencer will be able to unlock many doors of the inner philosophical conceptions of the great English philosopher, whose work shows the results of the preparation of his previous incarnations. His teachings regarding Evolution and Rhythm are in almost perfect agreement with the Hermetic Teachings regarding the Principle of Rhythm.

So, the student of Hermetics need not lay aside any of his cherished scientific views regarding the Universe. All he is asked to do is to grasp the underlying principle of "THE ALL is Mind; the Universe is Mental--held in the mind of THE ALL." He will find that the other six of the Seven Principles will "fit into" his scientific knowledge, and will serve to bring out obscure points and to throw light in dark corners. This is not to be wondered at, when we realize the influence of the Hermetic thought of the early philosophers of Greece, upon whose foundations of thought the theories of modern science largely rest. The acceptance of the First Hermetic Principle (Mentalism) is the only great point of difference between Modern Science and Hermetic students, and Science is gradually moving toward the Hermetic position in its groping in the dark for a way out of the Labyrinth into which it has wandered in its search for Reality.

The purpose of this lesson is to impress upon the minds of our students the fact that, to all intents and purposes, the Universe and its laws, and its phenomena, are just as REAL, so far as Man is

The Divine Paradox

concerned, as they would be under the hypotheses of Materialism or Energism. Under any hypothesis the Universe in its outer aspect is changing, ever-flowing, and transitory--and therefore devoid of substantiality and reality. But (note the other pole of the truth) under the same hypotheses, we are compelled to ACT AND LIVE as if the fleeting things were real and substantial. With this difference, always, between the various hypotheses--that under the old views Mental Power was ignored as a Natural Force, while under Mentalism it becomes the Greatest Natural Force. And this one difference revolutionizes Life, to those who understand the Principle and its resulting laws and practice.

So, finally, students all, grasp the advantage of Mentalism, and learn to know, use and apply the laws resulting therefrom. But do not yield to the temptation which, as The Kybalion states, overcomes the half-wise and which causes them to be hypnotized by the apparent unreality of things, the consequence being that they wander about like dream-people dwelling in a world of dreams, ignoring the practical work and life of man, the end being that "they are broken against the rocks and torn asunder by the elements, by reason of their folly." Rather follow the example of the wise, which the same authority states, "use Law against Laws; the higher against the lower; and by the Art of Alchemy transmute that which is undesirable into that which is worthy, and thus triumph." Following the authority, let us avoid the half-wisdom (which is folly) which ignores the truth that: "Mastery consists not in abnormal dreams, visions, and fantastic imaginings or living, but in using the higher forces against the lower--escaping the pains of the lower planes by vibrating on the higher." Remember always, student, that "Transmutation, not presumptuous denial, is the weapon of the Master." The above quotations are from The Kybalion, and are worthy of being committed to memory by the student.

The Kybalion

We do not live in a world of dreams, but in an Universe which while relative, is real so far as our lives and actions are concerned. Our business in the Universe is not to deny its existence, but to LIVE, using the Laws to rise from lower to higher--living on, doing the best that we can under the circumstances arising each day, and living, so far as is possible, to our biggest ideas and ideals. The true Meaning of Life is not known to men on this plane .if, indeed, to any--but the highest authorities, and our own intuitions, teach us that we will make no mistake in living up to the best that is in us, so far as is possible, and realising the Universal tendency in the same direction in spite of apparent evidence to the contrary. We are all on The Path--and the road leads upward ever, with frequent resting places.

Read the message of The Kybalion--and follow the example of "the wise"--avoiding the mistake of "the half-wise" who perish by reason of their folly.

CHAPTER VII

"THE ALL" IN ALL

"While All is in THE ALL, it is equally true that THE ALL is in ALL. To him who truly understands this truth hath come great knowledge."--The Kybalion.

How often have the majority of people heard repeated the statement that their Deity (called by many names) was "All in All" and how little have they suspected the inner occult truth concealed by these carelessly uttered words? The commonly used expression is a survival of the ancient Hermetic Maxim quoted above. As the Kybalion says: "To him who truly understands this truth, hath come great knowledge." And, this being so, let us seek this truth, the understanding of which means so much. In this statement of truth--this Hermetic Maxim--is concealed one of the greatest philosophical, scientific and religious truths.

We have given you the Hermetic Teaching regarding the Mental Nature of the Universe--the truth that "the Universe is Mental--held in the Mind of THE ALL." As the Kybalion says, in the passage quoted above: "All is in THE ALL." But note also the co-related statement, that: "It is equally true that THE ALL is in ALL." This apparently contradictory statement is reconcilable under the Law of Paradox. It is, moreover, an exact Hermetic statement of the relations existing between THE ALL and its Mental Universe. We have seen how "All is in THE ALL"--now let us examine the other aspect of the subject.

The Hermetic Teachings are to the effect that THE ALL is Imminent in ("remaining within; inherent; abiding within") its Universe, and in every part, particle, unit, or combination, within the Universe. This statement is usually illustrated by the Teachers by a reference to the Principle of Correspondence. The Teacher

The Kybalion

instructs the student to form a Mental Image of something, a person, an idea, something having a mental form, the favorite example being that of the author or dramatist forming an idea of his characters; or a painter or sculptor forming an image of an ideal that he wishes to express by his art. In each case, the student will find that while the image has its existence, and being, solely within his own mind, yet he, the student, author, dramatist, painter, or sculptor, is, in a sense, immanent in; remaining within; or abiding within, the mental image also. In other words, the entire virtue, life, spirit, of reality in the mental image is derived from the "immanent mind" of the thinker. Consider this for a moment, until the idea is grasped.

To take a modern example, let us say that Othello, Iago, Hamlet, Lear, Richard III, existed merely in the mind of Shakespeare, at the time of their conception or creation. And yet, Shakespeare also existed within each of these characters, giving them their vitality, spirit, and action. Whose is the "spirit" of the characters that we know as Micawber, Oliver Twist, Uriah Heep--is it Dickens, or have each of these characters a personal spirit, independent of their creator? Have the Venus of Medici, the Sistine Madonna, the Apollo Belvidere, spirits and reality of their own, or do they represent the spiritual and mental power of their creators? The Law of Paradox explains that both propositions are true, viewed from the proper viewpoints. Micawber is both Micawber, and yet Dickens. And, again, while Micawber may be said to be Dickens, yet Dickens is not identical with Micawber. Man, like Micawber, may exclaim: "The Spirit of my Creator is inherent within me-- and yet I am not HE!" How different this from the shocking half-truth so vociferously announced by certain of the half-wise, who fill the air with their raucous cries of: "I am God!" Imagine poor Micawber, or the sneaky Uriah Heep, crying: "I Am Dickens"; or some of the lowly clods in one of Shakespeare's plays, eloquently announcing that: "I Am Shakespeare!" THE ALL is in the earthworm, and yet

"The All" in All

the earth-worm is far from being THE ALL. And still the wonder remains, that though the earth-worm exists merely as a lowly thing, created and having its being solely within the Mind of THE ALL--yet THE ALL is immanent in the earthworm, and in the particles that go to make up the earth-worm. Can there be any greater mystery than this of "All in THE ALL; and THE ALL in All?"

The student will, of course, realize that the illustrations given above are necessarily imperfect and inadequate, for they represent the creation of mental images in finite minds, while the Universe is a creation of Infinite Mind--and the difference between the two poles separates them. And yet it is merely a matter of degree--the same Principle is in operation--the Principle of Correspondence manifests in each--"As above, so Below; as Below, so above."

And, in the degree that Man realizes the existence of the Indwelling Spirit immanent within his being, so will he rise in the spiritual scale of life. This is what spiritual development means--the recognition, realization, and manifestation of the Spirit within us. Try to remember this last definition--that of spiritual development. It contains the Truth of True Religion.

There are many planes of Being--many sub-planes of Life--many degrees of existence in the Universe. And all depend upon the advancement of beings in the scale, of which scale the lowest point is the grossest matter, the highest being separated only by the thinnest division from the SPIRIT of THE ALL. And, upward and onward along this Scale of Life, everything is moving. All are on the Path, whose end is THE ALL. All progress is a Returning Home. All is Upward and Onward, in spite of all seemingly contradictory appearances. Such is the message of the Illumined.

The Hermetic Teachings concerning the process of the Mental Creation of the Universe, are that at the beginning of the Creative

The Kybalion

Cycle, THE ALL, in its aspect of Being, projects its Will toward its aspect of "Becoming" and the process of creation begins. It is taught that the process consists of the lowering of Vibration until a very low degree of vibratory energy is reached, at which point the grossest possible form of Matter is manifested. This process is called the stage of Involution, in which THE ALL becomes "involved," or "wrapped up," in its creation. This process is believed by the Hermetists to have a Correspondence to the mental process of an artist, writer, or inventor, who becomes so wrapped up in his mental creation as to almost forget his own existence and who, for the time being, almost "lives in his creation," If instead of "wrapped" we use the word "rapt," perhaps we will give a better idea of what is meant.

This Involuntary stage of Creation is sometimes called the "Outpouring" of the Divine Energy, just as the Evolutionary state is called the "Indrawing." The extreme pole of the Creative process is considered to be the furthest removed from THE ALL, while the beginning of the Evolutionary stage is regarded as the beginning of the return swing of the pendulum of Rhythm--a "coming home" idea being held in all of the Hermetic Teachings.

The Teachings are that during the "Outpouring," the vibrations become lower and lower until finally the urge ceases, and the return swing begins. But there is this difference, that while in the "Outpouring" the creative forces manifest compactly and as a whole, yet from the beginning of the Evolutionary or "Indrawing" stage, there is manifested the Law of Individualization--that is, the tendency to separate into Units of Force, so that finally that which left THE ALL as unindividualized energy returns to its source as countless highly developed Units of Life, having risen higher and higher in the scale by means of Physical, Mental and Spiritual Evolution.

"The All" in All

The ancient Hermetists use the word "Meditation" in describing the process of the mental creation of the Universe in the Mind of THE ALL, the word "Contemplation" also being frequently employed. But the idea intended seems to be that of the employment of the Divine Attention. "Attention" is a word derived from the Latin root, meaning "to reach out; to stretch out," and so the act of Attention is really a mental "reaching out; extension" of mental energy, so that the underlying idea is readily understood when we examine into the real meaning of "Attention."

The Hermetic Teachings regarding the process of Evolution are that, THE ALL, having meditated upon the beginning of the Creation--having thus established the material foundations of the Universe--having thought it into existence--then gradually awakens or rouses from its Meditation and in so doing starts into manifestation the process of Evolution, on the material mental and spiritual planes, successively and in order. Thus the upward movement begins--and all begins to move Spiritward. Matter becomes less gross; the Units spring into being; the combinations begin to form; Life appears and manifests in higher and higher forms; and Mind becomes more and more in evidence--the vibrations constantly becoming higher. In short, the entire process of Evolution, in all of its phases, begins, and proceeds according to the established "Laws of the Indrawing" process. All of this occupies aeons upon aeons of Man's time, each aeon containing countless millions of years, but yet the Illumined inform us that the entire creation, including Involution and Evolution, of an Universe, is but "as the twinkle of the eye" to THE ALL. At the end of countless cycles of aeons of time, THE ALL withdraws its Attention--its Contemplation and Meditation--of the Universe, for the Great Work is finished--and All is withdrawn into THE ALL from which it emerged. But Mystery of Mysteries--the Spirit of each soul is not annihilated, but is infinitely expanded--the

Created and the Creator are merged. Such is the report of the Illumined!

The above illustration of the "meditation," and subsequent "awakening from meditation," of THE ALL, is of course but an attempt of the teachers to describe the Infinite process by a finite example. And, yet: "As Below, so Above." The difference is merely in degree. And just as THE ALL arouses itself from the meditation upon the Universe, so does Man (in time) cease from manifesting upon the Material Plane, and withdraws himself more and more into the Indwelling Spirit, which is indeed "The Divine Ego."

There is one more matter of which we desire to speak in this lesson, and that comes very near to an invasion of the Metaphysical field of speculation, although our purpose is merely to show the futility of such speculation. We allude to the question which inevitably comes to the mind of all thinkers who have ventured to seek the Truth. The question is: "WHY does THE ALL create Universes" The question may be asked in different forms, but the above is the gist of the inquiry.

Men have striven hard to answer this question, but still there is no answer worthy of the name. Some have imagined that THE ALL had something to gain by it, but this is absurd, for what could THE ALL gain that it did not already possess? Others have sought the answer in the idea that THE ALL "wished something to love" and others that it created for pleasure, or amusement; or because it "was lonely" or to manifest its power;--all puerile explanations and ideas, belonging to the childish period of thought.

Others have sought to explain the mystery by assuming that THE ALL found itself "compelled" to create, by reason of its own "internal nature"--its "creative instinct." This idea is in advance of the others, but its weak point lies in the idea of THE ALL being "compelled" by anything, internal or external. If its "internal

"The All" in All

nature," or "creative instinct," compelled it to do anything, then the "internal nature" or "creative instinct" would be the Absolute, instead of THE ALL, and so accordingly that part of the proposition falls. And, yet, THE ALL does create and manifest, and seems to find some kind of satisfaction in so doing. And it is difficult to escape the conclusion that in some infinite degree it must have what would correspond to an "inner nature," or "creative instinct," in man, with correspondingly infinite Desire and Will. It could not act unless it Willed to Act; and it would not Will to Act, unless it Desired to Act and it would not Desire to Act unless it obtained some Satisfaction thereby. And all of these things would belong to an "Inner Nature," and might be postulated as existing according to the Law of Correspondence. But, still, we prefer to think of THE ALL as acting entirely FREE from any influence, internal as well as external. That is the problem which lies at the root of difficulty--and the difficulty that lies at the root of the problem.

Strictly speaking, there cannot be said to be any "Reason" whatsoever for THE ALL to act, for a "reason" implies a "cause," and THE ALL is above Cause and Effect, except when it Wills to become a Cause, at which time the Principle is set into motion. So, you see, the matter is Unthinkable, just as THE ALL is Unknowable. Just as we say THE ALL merely "IS"--so we are compelled to say that "THE ALL ACTS BECAUSE IT ACTS." At the last, THE ALL is All Reason in Itself; All Law in Itself; All Action in Itself--and it may be said, truthfully, that THE ALL is Its Own Reason; its own Law; its own Act--or still further, that THE ALL; Its Reason; Its Act; is Law; are ONE, all being names for the same thing. In the opinion of those who are giving you these present lessons, the answer is locked up in the INNER SELF of THE ALL, along with its Secret of Being. The Law of Correspondence, in our opinion, reaches only to that aspect of THE ALL, which may be spoken of as "The Aspect of BECOMING."

Back of that Aspect is "The Aspect of BEING" in which all Laws are lost in LAW; all Principles merge into PRINCIPLE--and THE ALL; PRINCIPLE; and BEING; are IDENTICAL, ONE AND THE SAME. Therefore, Metaphysical speculation on this point is futile. We go into the matter here, merely to show that we recognize the question, and also the absurdity of the ordinary answers of metaphysics and theology.

In conclusion, it may be of interest to our students to learn that while some of the ancient, and modern, Hermetic Teachers have rather inclined in the direction of applying the Principle of Correspondence to the question, with the result of the "Inner Nature" conclusion,--still the legends have it that HERMES, the Great, when asked this question by his advanced students, answered them by PRESSING HIS LIPS TIGHTLY TOGETHER and saying not a word, indicating that there WAS NO ANSWER. But, then, he may have intended to apply the axiom of his philosophy, that: "The lips of Wisdom are closed, except to the ears of Understanding," believing that even his advanced students did not possess the Understanding which entitled them to the Teaching. At any rate, if Hermes possessed the Secret, he failed to impart it, and so far as the world is concerned THE LIPS OF HERMES ARE CLOSED regarding it. And where the Great Hermes hesitated to speak, what mortal may dare to teach?

But, remember, that whatever be the answer to this problem, if indeed there be an answer the truth remains that: "While All is in THE ALL, it is equally true that THE ALL is in All." The Teaching on this point is emphatic. And, we may add the concluding words of the quotation: "To him who truly understands this truth, hath come great knowledge."

CHAPTER VIII

PLANES OF CORRESPONDENCE

"As above, so below; as below, so above."--The Kybalion.

The great Second Hermetic Principle embodies the truth that there is a harmony, agreement, and correspondence between the several planes of Manifestation, Life and Being. This truth is a truth because all that is included in the Universe emanates from the same source, and the same laws, principles, and characteristics apply to each unit, or combination of units, of activity, as each manifests its own phenomena upon its own plane.

For the purpose of convenience of thought and study, the Hermetic Philosophy considers that the Universe may be divided into three great classes of phenomena, known as the Three Great Planes, namely:

1. The Great Physical Plane.
2. The Great Mental Plane.
3. The Great Spiritual Plane.

These divisions are more or less artificial and arbitrary, for the truth is that all of the three divisions are but ascending degrees of the great scale of Life, the lowest point of which is undifferentiated Matter, and the highest point that of Spirit. And, moreover, the different Planes shade into each other, so that no hard and fast division may be made between the higher phenomena of the Physical and the lower of the Mental; or between the higher of the Mental and the lower of the Physical.

In short, the Three Great Planes may be regarded as three great groups of degrees of Life Manifestation. While the purposes of this little book do not allow us to enter into an extended discussion of,

The Kybalion

or explanation of, the subject of these different planes, still we think it well to give a general description of the same at this point.

At the beginning we may as well consider the question so often asked by the neophyte, who desires to be informed regarding the meaning of the word "Plane", which term has been very freely used, and very poorly explained, in many recent works upon the subject of occultism. The question is generally about as follows: "Is a Plane a place having dimensions, or is it merely a condition or state?" We answer: "No, not a place, nor ordinary dimension of space; and yet more than a state or condition. It may be considered as a state or condition, and yet the state or condition is a degree of dimension, in a scale subject to measurement." Somewhat paradoxical, is it not? But let us examine the matter. A "dimension," you know, is "a measure in a straight line, relating to measure," etc. The ordinary dimensions of space are length, breadth, and height, or perhaps length, breadth, height, thickness or circumference. But there is another dimension of "created things" or "measure in a straight line," known to occultists, and to scientists as well, although the latter have not as yet applied the term "dimension" to it--and this new dimension, which, by the way, is the much speculated -about "Fourth Dimension," is the standard used in determining the degrees or "planes."

This Fourth Dimension may be called "The Dimension of Vibration" It is a fact well known to modern science, as well as to the Hermetists who have embodied the truth in their "Third Hermetic Principle," that "everything is in motion; everything vibrates; nothing is at rest." From the highest manifestation, to the lowest, everything and all things Vibrate. Not only do they vibrate at different rates of motion, but as in different directions and in a different manner. The degrees of the rate of vibrations constitute the degrees of measurement on the Scale of Vibrations--in other words the degrees of the Fourth Dimension. And these degrees

Planes of Correspondence

form what occultists call "Planes" The higher the degree of rate of vibration, the higher the plane, and the higher the manifestation of Life occupying that plane. So that while a plane is not "a place," nor yet "a state or condition," yet it possesses qualities common to both. We shall have more to say regarding the subject of the scale of Vibrations in our next lessons, in which we shall consider the Hermetic Principle of Vibration.

You will kindly remember, however, that the Three Great Planes are not actual divisions of the phenomena of the Universe, but merely arbitrary terms used by the Hermetists in order to aid in the thought and study of the various degrees and Forms of universal activity and life. The atom of matter, the unit of force, the mind of man, and the being of the arch -angel are all but degrees in one scale, and all fundamentally the same, the difference between solely a matter of degree, and rate of vibration--all are creations of THE ALL, and have their existence solely within the Infinite Mind of THE ALL.

The Hermetists sub-divide each of the Three Great Planes into Seven Minor Planes, and each of these latter are also sub-divided into seven sub-planes, all divisions being more or less arbitrary, shading into each other, and adopted merely for convenience of scientific study and thought.

The Great Physical Plane, and its Seven Minor Planes, is that division of the phenomena of the Universe which includes all that relates to physics, or material things, forces, and manifestations. It includes all forms of that which we call Matter, and all forms of that which we call Energy or Force. But you must remember that the Hermetic Philosophy does not recognize Matter as a thing in itself, or as having a separate existence even in the Mind of THE ALL. The Teachings are that Matter is but a form of Energy--.that is, Energy at a low rate of vibrations of a certain kind. And accordingly the Hermetists classify Matter under the head of

Energy, and give to it three of the Seven Minor Planes of the Great Physical Plane.

These Seven Minor Physical Planes are as follows:

1. The Plane of Matter (A)
2. The Plane of Matter (B)
3. The Plane of Matter (C)
4. The Plane of Ethereal Substance
5. The Plane of Energy (A)
6. The Plane of Energy (B)
7. The Plane of Energy (C)

The Plane of Matter (A) comprises the forms of Matter in its form of solids, liquids, and gases, as generally recognized by the text-books on physics. The Plane of Matter (B) comprises certain higher and more subtle forms of Matter of the existence of which modern science is but now recognizing, the phenomena of Radiant Matter, in its phases of radium, etc., belonging to the lower sub-division of this Minor Plane. The Plane of Matter (C) comprises forms of the most subtle and tenuous Matter, the existence of which is not suspected by ordinary scientists. The Plane of Ethereal Substance comprises that which science speaks of as "The Ether", a substance of extreme tenuity and elasticity, pervading all Universal Space, and acting as a medium for the transmission of waves of energy, such as light, heat, electricity, etc. This Ethereal Substance forms a connecting link between Matter (so-called) and Energy, and partakes of the nature of each. The Hermetic Teachings, however, instruct that this plane has seven sub-divisions (as have all of the Minor Planes), and that in fact there are seven ethers, instead of but one.

Next above the Plane of Ethereal Substance comes the Plane of Energy (A), which comprises the ordinary forms of Energy known to science, its seven sub-planes being, respectively, Heat; Light;

Planes of Correspondence

Magnetism; Electricity, and Attraction (including Gravitation, Cohesion, Chemical Affinity, etc.) and several other forms of energy indicated by scientific experiments but not as yet named or classified. The Plane of Energy (B) comprises seven subplanes of higher forms of energy not as yet discovered by science, but which have been called "Nature's Finer Forces" and which are called into operation in manifestations of certain forms of mental phenomena, and by which such phenomena becomes possible. The Plane of Energy (C) comprises seven sub-planes of energy so highly organized that it bears many of the characteristics of "life," but which is not recognized by the minds of men on the ordinary plane of development, being available for the use on beings of the Spiritual Plane alone--such energy is unthinkable to ordinary man, and may be considered almost as "the divine power." The beings employing the same are as "gods" compared even to the highest human types known to us.

The Great Mental Plane comprises those forms of "living things" known to us in ordinary life, as well as certain other forms not so well known except to the occultist. The classification of the Seven Minor Mental Planes is more or less satisfactory and arbitrary (unless accompanied by elaborate explanations which are foreign to the purpose of this particular work), but we may as well mention them. They are as follows:

1. The Plane of Mineral Mind
2. The Plane of Elemental Mind (A)
3. The Plane of Plant Mind
4. The Plane of Elemental Mind (B)
5. The Plane of Animal Mind
6. The Plane of Elemental Mind (C)
7. The Plane of Human Mind

The Plane of Mineral Mind comprises the "states or conditions" of the units or entities, or groups and combinations of the same,

The Kybalion

which animate the forms known to us as "minerals, chemicals, etc." These entities must not be confounded with the molecules, atoms and corpuscles themselves, the latter being merely the material bodies or forms of these entities, just as a man's body is but his material form and not "himself." These entities may be called "souls" in one sense, and are living beings of a low degree of development, life, and mind--just a little more than the units of "living energy" which comprise the higher sub-divisions of the highest Physical Plane. The average mind does not generally attribute the possession of mind, soul, or life, to the mineral kingdom, but all occultists recognize the existence of the same, and modern science is rapidly moving forward to the point-of-view of the Hermetic, in this respect. The molecules, atoms and corpuscles have their "loves and hates"; "likes and dislikes"; "attractions and repulsions". "affinities and non-affinities," etc., and some of the more daring of modern scientific minds have expressed the opinion that the desire and will, emotions and feelings, of the atoms differ only in degree from those of men. We have no time or space to argue this matter here. All occultists know it to be a fact, and others are referred to some of the more recent scientific works for outside corroboration. There are the usual seven sub-divisions to this plane.

The Plane of Elemental Mind (A) comprises the state or condition, and degree of mental and vital development of a class of entities unknown to the average man, but recognized to occultists. They are invisible to the ordinary senses of man, but, nevertheless, exist and play their part of the Drama of the Universe. Their degree of intelligence is between that of the mineral and chemical entities on the one hand, and of the entities of the plant kingdom on the other. There are seven subdivisions to this plane, also.

The Plane of Plant Mind, in its seven sub-divisions, comprises the states or conditions of the entities comprising the kingdoms of the

Planes of Correspondence

Plant World, the vital and mental phenomena of which is fairly well understood by the average intelligent person, many new and interesting scientific works regarding "Mind and Life in Plants" having been published during the last decade. Plants have life, mind and "souls," as well as have the animals, man, and super-man.

The Plane of Elemental Mind (B), in its seven sub-divisions, comprises the states and conditions of a higher form of "elemental" or unseen entities, playing their part in the general work of the Universe, the mind and life of which form a part of the scale between the Plane of Plant Mind and the Plane of Animal Mind, the entities partaking of the nature of both.

The Plane of Animal Mind, in its seven sub-divisions, comprises the states and conditions of the entities, beings, or souls, animating the animal forms of life, familiar to us all. It is not necessary to go into details regarding this kingdom or plane of life, for the animal world is as familiar to us as is our own.

The Plane of Elemental Mind (C), in its seven sub-divisions, comprises those entities or beings, invisible as are all such elemental forms, which partake of the nature of both animal and human life in a degree and in certain combinations. The highest forms are semi-human in intelligence.

The Plane of Human Mind, in its seven sub-divisions, comprises those manifestations of life and mentality which are common to Man, in his various grades, degrees, and divisions. In this connection, we wish to point out the fact that the average man of today occupies but the fourth sub-division of the Plane of Human Mind, and only the most intelligent have crossed the borders of the Fifth Sub-Division. It has taken the race millions of years to reach this stage, and it will take many more years for the race to move on to the sixth and seventh sub-divisions, and beyond. But, remember, that there have been races before us which have passed through these degrees, and then on to higher planes. Our own race is the fifth (with stragglers from the fourth) which has set foot upon The Path. And, then there are a few advanced souls of our own race who have outstripped the masses, and who have passed on to the sixth and seventh sub-division, and some few being still further on. The man of the Sixth Sub-Division will be "The Super-Man"; he of the Seventh will be "The Over-Man."

In our consideration of the Seven Minor Mental Planes, we have merely referred to the Three Elementary Planes in a general way. We do not wish to go into this subject in detail in this work, for it does not belong to this part of the general philosophy and teachings. But we may say this much, in order to give you a little clearer idea, of the relations of these planes to the more familiar ones--the Elementary Planes bear the same relation to the Planes of Mineral, Plant, Animal and Human Mentality and Life, that the black keys on the piano do to the white keys. The white keys are sufficient to produce music, but there are certain scales, melodies, and harmonies, in which the black keys play their part, and in which their presence is necessary. They are also necessary as "connecting links" of soul-condition; entity states, etc., between the several other planes, certain forms of development being attained therein--this last fact giving to the reader who can "read between the lines" a new light upon the processes of Evolution, and a new key to the secret door of the "leaps of life" between kingdom and kingdom. The great kingdoms of Elementals are fully recognized by all occultists, and the esoteric writings are full of mention of them. The readers of Bulwer's "Sanoni" and similar tales will recognize the entities inhabiting these planes of life.

Passing on from the Great Mental Plane to the Great Spiritual Plane, what shall we say? How can we explain these higher states of Being, Life and Mind, to minds as yet unable to grasp and

Planes of Correspondence

understand the higher subdivisions of the Plane of Human Mind? The task is impossible. We can speak only in the most general terms. How may Light be described to a man born blind--how sugar, to a man who has never tasted anything sweet--how harmony, to one born deaf?

All that we can say is that the Seven Minor Planes of the Great Spiritual Plane (each Minor Plane having its seven sub-divisions) comprise Beings possessing Life, Mind and Form as far above that of Man of to-day as the latter is above the earth-worm, mineral or even certain forms of Energy or Matter. The Life of these Beings so far transcends ours, that we cannot even think of the details of the same; their minds so far transcend ours, that to them we scarcely seem to "think," and our mental processes seem almost akin to material processes; the Matter of which their forms are composed is of the highest Planes of Matter, nay, some are even said to be "clothed in Pure Energy." What may be said of such Beings?

On the Seven Minor Planes of the Great Spiritual Plane exist Beings of whom we may speak as Angels; Archangels; Demi-Gods. On the lower Minor Planes dwell those great souls whom we call Masters and Adepts. Above them come the Great Hierarchies of the Angelic Hosts, unthinkable to man; and above those come those who may without irreverence be called "The Gods," so high in the scale of Being are they, their being, intelligence and power being akin to those attributed by the races of men to their conceptions of Deity. These Beings are beyond even the highest flights of the human imagination, the word "Divine" being the only one applicable to them. Many of these Beings, as well as the Angelic Host, take the greatest interest in the affairs of the Universe and play an important part in its affairs. These Unseen Divinities and Angelic Helpers extend their influence freely and powerfully, in the process of Evolution, and Cosmic Progress. Their occasional intervention and assistance in human affairs have led to the many legends, beliefs, religions and traditions of the race, past and present. They have superimposed their knowledge and power upon the world, again and again, all under the Law of THE ALL, of course.

But, yet, even the highest of these advanced Beings exist merely as creations of, and in, the Mind of THE ALL, and are subject to the Cosmic Processes and Universal Laws. They are still Mortal. We may call them "gods" if we like, but still they are but the Elder Brethren of the Race,--the advanced souls who have outstripped their brethren, and who have foregone the ecstasy of Absorption by THE ALL, in order to help the race on its upward journey along The Path. But, they belong to the Universe, and are subject to its conditions--they are mortal--and their plane is below that of Absolute Spirit.

Only the most advanced Hermetists are able to grasp the Inner Teachings regarding the state of existence, and the powers manifested on the Spiritual Planes. The phenomena is so much higher than that of the Mental Planes that a confusion of ideas would surely result from an attempt to describe the same. Only those whose minds have been carefully trained along the lines of the Hermetic Philosophy for years--yes, those who have brought with them from other incarnations the knowledge acquired previously--can comprehend just what is meant by the Teaching regarding these Spiritual Planes. And much of these Inner Teachings is held by the Hermetists as being too sacred, important and even dangerous for general public dissemination. The intelligent student may recognize what we mean by this when we state that the meaning of "Spirit" as used by the Hermetists is akin to "Living Power"; "Animated Force;" "Inner Essence;" "Essence of Life," etc., which meaning must not be confounded with that usually and commonly employed in connection with the term, i.e., "religious; ecclesiastical; spiritual; ethereal; holy," etc., etc. To

Planes of Correspondence

occultists the word "Spirit" is used in the sense of "The Animating Principle," carrying with it the idea of Power, Living Energy, Mystic Force, etc. And occultists know that that which is known to them as "Spiritual Power" may be employed for evil as well as good ends (in accordance with the Principle of Polarity), a fact which has been recognized by the majority of religions in their conceptions of Satan, Beelzebub, the Devil, Lucifer, Fallen Angels, etc. And so the knowledge regarding these Planes has been kept in the Holy of Holies in all Esoteric Fraternities and Occult Orders,-- in the Secret Chamber of the Temple. But this may be said here, that those who have attained high spiritual powers and have misused them, have a terrible fate in store for them, and the swing of the pendulum of Rhythm will inevitably swing them back to the furthest extreme of Material existence, from which point they must retrace their steps Spiritward, along the weary rounds of The Path, but always with the added torture of having always with them a lingering memory of the heights from which they fell owing to their evil actions. The legends of the Fallen Angels have a basis in actual facts, as all advanced occultists know. The striving for selfish power on the Spiritual Planes inevitably results in the selfish soul losing its spiritual balance and falling back as far as it had previously risen. But to even such a soul, the opportunity of a return is given--and such souls make the return journey, paying the terrible penalty according to the invariable Law.

In conclusion we would again remind you that according to the Principle of Correspondence, which embodies the truth: "As Above so Below; as Below, so Above," all of the Seven Hermetic Principles are in full operation on all of the many planes, Physical Mental and Spiritual. The Principle of Mental Substance of course applies to all the planes, for all are held in the Mind of THE ALL. The Principle of Correspondence manifests in all, for there is a correspondence, harmony and agreement between the several planes. The Principle of Vibration manifests on all planes, in fact the very differences that go to make the "planes" arise from Vibration, as we have explained. The Principle of Polarity manifests on each plane, the extremes of the Poles being apparently opposite and contradictory. The Principle of Rhythm manifests on each Plane, the movement of the phenomena having its ebb and flow, rise and flow, incoming and outgoing. The Principle of Cause and Effect manifests on each Plane, every Effect having its Cause and every Cause having its effect. The Principle of Gender manifests on each Plane, the Creative Energy being always manifest, and operating along the lines of its Masculine and Feminine Aspects.

"As Above so Below; as Below, so Above." This centuries old Hermetic axiom embodies one of the great Principles of Universal Phenomena. As we proceed with our consideration of the remaining Principles, we will see even more clearly the truth of the universal nature of this great Principle of Correspondence.

CHAPTER IX

VIBRATION

"Nothing rests; everything moves; everything vibrates."--The Kybalion.

The great Third Hermetic Principle--the Principle of Vibration--embodies the truth that Motion is manifest in everything in the Universe--that nothing is at rest--that everything moves, vibrates, and circles. This Hermetic Principle was recognized by some of the early Greek philosophers who embodied it in their systems. But, then, for centuries it was lost sight of by the thinkers outside of the Hermetic ranks. But in the Nineteenth Century physical science rediscovered the truth and the Twentieth Century scientific discoveries have added additional proof of the correctness and truth of this centuries-old Hermetic doctrine.

The Hermetic Teachings are that not only is everything in constant movement and vibration, but that the "differences" between the various manifestations of the universal power are due entirely to the varying rate and mode of vibrations. Not only this, but that even THE ALL, in itself, manifests a constant vibration of such an infinite degree of intensity and rapid motion that it may be practically considered as at rest, the teachers directing the attention of the students to the fact that even on the physical plane a rapidly moving object (such as a revolving wheel) seems to be at rest. The Teachings are to the effect that Spirit is at one end of the Pole of Vibration, the other Pole being certain extremely gross forms of Matter. Between these two poles are millions upon millions of different rates and modes of vibration.

Modern Science has proven that all that we call Matter and Energy are but "modes of vibratory motion," and some of the more advanced scientists are rapidly moving toward the positions of the occultists who hold that the phenomena of Mind are likewise modes of vibration or motion. Let us see what science has to say regarding the question of vibrations in matter and energy.

In the first place, science teaches that all matter manifests, in some degree, the vibrations arising from temperature or heat. Be an object cold or hot--both being but degrees of the same things--it manifests certain heat vibrations, and in that sense is in motion and vibration. Then all particles of Matter are in circular movement, from corpuscle to suns. The planets revolve around suns, and many of them turn on their axes. The suns move around greater central points, and these are believed to move around still greater, and so on, ad infinitum. The molecules of which the particular kinds of Matter are composed are in a state of constant vibration and movement around each other and against each other. The molecules are composed of Atoms, which, likewise, are in a state of constant movement and vibration. The atoms are composed of Corpuscles, sometimes called "electrons," "ions," etc., which also are in a state of rapid motion, revolving around each other, and which manifest a very rapid state and mode of vibration. And, so we see that all forms of Matter manifest Vibration, in accordance with the Hermetic Principle of Vibration.

And so it is with the various forms of Energy. Science teaches that Light, Heat, Magnetism and Electricity are but forms of vibratory motion connected in some way with, and probably emanating from the Ether. Science does not as yet attempt to explain the nature of the phenomena known as Cohesion, which is the principle of Molecular Attraction; nor Chemical Affinity, which is the principle of Atomic Attraction; nor Gravitation (the greatest mystery of the three), which is the principle of attraction by which every particle or mass of Matter is bound to every other particle or mass. These three forms of Energy are not as yet understood by science, yet the writers incline to the opinion that these too are

Vibration

manifestations of some form of vibratory energy, a fact which the Hermetists have held and taught for ages past.

The Universal Ether, which is postulated by science without its nature being understood clearly, is held by the Hermetists to be but a higher manifestation of that which is erroneously called matter--that is to say, Matter at a higher degree of vibration--and is called by them "The Ethereal Substance." The Hermetists teach that this Ethereal Substance is of extreme tenuity and elasticity, and pervades universal space, serving as a medium of transmission of waves of vibratory energy, such as heat, light, electricity, magnetism, etc. The Teachings are that The Ethereal Substance is a connecting link between the forms of vibratory energy known as "Matter" on the one hand, and "Energy or Force" on the other; and also that it manifests a degree of vibration, in rate and mode, entirely its own.

Scientists have offered the illustration of a rapidly moving wheel, top, or cylinder, to show the effects of increasing rates of vibration. The illustration supposes a wheel, top, or revolving cylinder, running at a low rate of speed--we will call this revolving thing "the object" in following out the illustration. Let us suppose the object moving slowly. It may be seen readily, but no sound of its movement reaches the ear. The speed is gradually increased. In a few moments its movement becomes so rapid that a deep growl or low note may be heard. Then as the rate is increased the note rises one in the musical scale. Then, the motion being still further increased, the next highest note is distinguished. Then, one after another, all the notes of the musical scale appear, rising higher and higher as the motion is increased. Finally when the motions have reached a certain rate the final note perceptible to human ears is reached and the shrill, piercing shriek dies away, and silence follows. No sound is heard from the revolving object, the rate of motion being so high that the human ear cannot register the vibrations. Then comes the perception of rising degrees of Heat. Then after quite a time the eye catches a glimpse of the object becoming a dull dark reddish color. As the rate increases, the red becomes brighter. Then as the speed is increased, the red melts into an orange. Then the orange melts into a yellow. Then follow, successively, the shades of green, blue, indigo, and finally violet, as the rate of sped increases. Then the violet shades away, and all color disappears, the human eye not being able to register them. But there are invisible rays emanating from the revolving object, the rays that are used in photographing, and other subtle rays of light. Then begin to manifest the peculiar rays known as the "X Rays," etc., as the constitution of the object changes. Electricity and Magnetism are emitted when the appropriate rate of vibration is attained.

When the object reaches a certain rate of vibration its molecules disintegrate, and resolve themselves into the original elements or atoms. Then the atoms, following the Principle of Vibration, are separated into the countless corpuscles of which they are composed. And finally, even the corpuscles disappear and the object may be said to Be composed of The Ethereal Substance. Science does not dare to follow the illustration further, but the Hermetists teach that if the vibrations be continually increased the object would mount up the successive states of manifestation and would in turn manifest the various mental stages, and then on Spiritward, until it would finally re-enter THE ALL, which is Absolute Spirit. The "object," however, would have ceased to be an "object" long before the stage of Ethereal Substance was reached, but otherwise the illustration is correct inasmuch as it shows the effect of constantly increased rates and modes of vibration. It must be remembered, in the above illustration, that at the stages at which the "object" throws off vibrations of light, heat, etc., it is not actually "resolved" into those forms of energy (which are much higher in the scale), but simply that it reaches a degree of vibration

Vibration

in which those forms of energy are liberated, in a degree, from the confining influences of its molecules, atoms and corpuscles, as the case may be. These forms of energy, although much higher in the scale than matter, are imprisoned and confined in the material combinations, by reason of the energies manifesting through, and using material forms, but thus becoming entangled and confined in their creations of material forms, which, to an extent, is true of all creations, the creating force becoming involved in its creation.

But the Hermetic Teachings go much further than do those of modern science. They teach that all manifestation of thought, emotion, reason, will or desire, or any mental state or condition, are accompanied by vibrations, a portion of which are thrown off and which tend to affect the minds of other persons by "induction." This is the principle which produces the phenomena of "telepathy"; mental influence, and other forms of the action and power of mind over mind, with which the general public is rapidly becoming acquainted, owing to the wide dissemination of occult knowledge by the various schools, cults and teachers along these lines at this time.

Every thought, emotion or mental state has its corresponding rate and mode of vibration. And by an effort of the will of the person, or of other persons, these mental states may be reproduced, just as a musical tone may be reproduced by causing an instrument to vibrate at a certain rate--just as color may be reproduced in the same may. By a knowledge of the Principle of Vibration, as applied to Mental Phenomena, one may polarize his mind at any degree he wishes, thus gaining a perfect control over his mental states, moods, etc. In the same way he may affect the minds of others, producing the desired mental states in them. In short, he may be able to produce on the Mental Plane that which science produces on the Physical Plane--namely, "Vibrations at Will." This power of course may be acquired only by the proper instruction, exercises, practice, etc., the science being that of Mental Transmutation, one of the branches of the Hermetic Art.

A little reflection on what we have said will show the student that the Principle of Vibration underlies the wonderful phenomena of the power manifested by the Masters and Adepts, who are able to apparently set aside the Laws of Nature, but who, in reality, are simply using one law against another; one principle against others; and who accomplish their results by changing the vibrations of material objects, or forms of energy, and thus perform what are commonly called "miracles."

As one of the old Hermetic writers has truly said: "He who understands the Principle of Vibration, has grasped the scepter of Power."

CHAPTER X

POLARITY

"Everything is dual; everything has poles; everything has its pair of opposites; like and unlike are the same; opposites are identical in nature, but different in degree; extremes meet; all truths are but half-truths; all paradoxes may be reconciled."--The Kybalion.

The great Fourth Hermetic Principle--the Principle of Polarity embodies the truth that all manifested things have "two sides"; "two aspects"; "two poles"; a "pair of opposites," with manifold degrees between the two extremes. The old paradoxes, which have ever perplexed the mind of men, are explained by an understanding of this Principle. Man has always recognized something akin to this Principle, and has endeavored to express it by such sayings, maxims and aphorisms as the following: "Everything is and isn't, at the same time"; "all truths are but half-truths"; "every truth is half-false"; "there are two sides to everything"--"there is a reverse side to every shield," etc., etc.

The Hermetic Teachings are to the effect that the difference between things seemingly diametrically opposed to each other is merely a matter of degree. It teaches that "the pairs of opposites may be reconciled," and that "thesis and anti-thesis are identical in nature, but different in degree"; and that the "universal reconciliation of opposites" is effected by a recognition of this Principle of Polarity. The teachers claim that illustrations of this Principle may be had on every hand, and from an examination into the real nature of anything. They begin by showing that Spirit and Matter are but the two poles of the same thing, the intermediate planes being merely degrees of vibration. They show that THE ALL and The Many are the same, the difference being merely a matter of degree of Mental Manifestation. Thus the LAW and Laws are the two opposite poles of one thing. Likewise, PRINCIPLE and Principles. Infinite Mind and finite minds.

Then passing on to the Physical Plane, they illustrate the Principle by showing that Heat and Cold are identical in nature, the differences being merely a matter of degrees. The thermometer shows many degrees of temperature, the lowest pole being called "cold," and the highest "heat." Between these two poles are many degrees of "heat" or "cold," call them either and you are equally correct. The higher of two degrees is always "warmer," while the lower is always "colder." There is no absolute standard-all is a matter of degree. There is no place on the thermometer where heat ceases and cold begins. It is all a matter of higher or lower vibrations. The very terms "high" and "low," which we are compelled to use, are but poles of the same thing-the terms are relative. So with "East and West"--travel around the world in an eastward direction, and you reach a point which is called west at your starting point, and you return from that westward point. Travel far enough North, and you will find yourself traveling South, or vice versa.

Light and Darkness are poles of the same thing, with many degrees between them. The musical scale is the same--starting with "C" you move upward until you reach another "C" and so on, the differences between the two ends of the board being the same, with many degrees between the two extremes. The scale of color is the same-higher and lower vibrations being the only difference between high violet and low red. Large and Small are relative. So are Noise and Quiet; Hard and Soft follow the rule. Likewise Sharp and Dull. Positive and Negative are two poles of the same thing, with countless degrees between them.

Good and Bad are not absolute--we call one end of the scale Good and the other Bad, or one end Good and the other Evil, according to the use of the terms. A thing is "less good" than the thing higher

Polarity

in the scale; but that "less good" thing, in turn, is "more good" than the thing next below it--and so on, the "more or less" being regulated by the position on the scale.

And so it is on the Mental Plane. "Love and. Hate" are generally regarded as being things diametrically opposed to each other; entirely different; unreconcilable. But we apply the Principle of Polarity; we find that there is no such thing as Absolute Love or Absolute Hate, as distinguished from each other. The two are merely terms applied to the two poles of the same thing. Beginning at any point of the scale we find "more love," or "less hate," as we ascend the scale; and "more hate" or "less love" as we descend this being true no matter from what point, high or low, we may start. There are degrees of Love and Hate, and there is a middle point where "Like and Dislike" become so faint that it is difficult to distinguish between them. Courage and Fear come under the same rule. The Pairs of Opposites exist everywhere. Where you find one thing you find its opposite-the two poles.

And it is this fact that enables the Hermetist to transmute one mental state into another, along the lines of Polarization. Things belonging to different classes cannot be transmuted into each other, but things of the same class may be changed, that is, may have their polarity changed. Thus Love never becomes East or West, or Red or Violet-but it may and often does turn into Hate and likewise Hate may be transformed into Love, by changing its polarity. Courage may be transmuted into Fear, and the reverse. Hard things may be rendered Soft. Dull things become Sharp. Hot things become Cold. And so on, the transmutation always being between things of the same kind of different degrees. Take the case of a Fearful man. By raising his mental vibrations along the line of Fear- Courage, he can be filled with the highest degree of Courage and Fearlessness. And, likewise, the Slothful man may change himself into an Active, Energetic individual simply by polarizing along the lines of the desired quality.

The student who is familiar with the processes by which the various schools of Mental Science, etc., produce changes in the mental states of those following their teachings, may not readily understand the principle underlying many of these changes. When, however, the Principle of Polarity is once grasped, and it is seen that the mental changes are occasioned by a change of polarity-a sliding along the same scale-the hatter is readily understood. The change is not in the nature of a transmutation of one thing into another thing entirely different-but is merely a change of degree in the same things, a vastly important difference. For instance, borrowing an analogy from the Physical Plane, it is impossible to change Heat into Sharpness, Loudness, Highness, etc., but Heat may readily be transmuted into Cold, simply by lowering the vibrations. In the same way Hate and Love are mutually transmutable; so are Fear and Courage. But Fear cannot be transformed into Love, nor can Courage be transmuted into Hate. The mental states belong to innumerable classes, each class of which has its opposite poles, along which transmutation is possible.

The student will readily recognize that in the mental states, as well as in the phenomena of the Physical Plane, the two poles may be classified as Positive and Negative, respectively. Thus Love is Positive to Hate; Courage to Fear; Activity to Non-Activity, etc., etc. And it will also be noticed that even to those unfamiliar with the Principle of Vibration, the Positive pole seems to be of a higher degree than the Negative, and readily dominates it. The tendency of Nature is in the direction of the dominant activity of the Positive pole.

In addition to the changing of the poles of one's own mental states by the operation of the art of Polarization, the phenomena of

Polarity

Mental Influence, in its manifold phases, shows us that the principle may be extended so as to embrace the phenomena of the influence of one mind over that of another, of which so much has been written and taught of late years. When it is understood that Mental Induction is possible, that is that mental states may be produced by "induction" from others, then we can readily see how a certain rate of vibration, or polarization of a certain mental state, may be communicated to another person, and his polarity in that class of mental states thus changed. It is along this principle that the results of many of the "mental treatments" are obtained. For instance, a person is "blue," melancholy and full of fear. A mental scientist bringing his own mind up to the desired vibration by his trained will, and thus obtaining the desired polarization in his own case, then produces a similar mental state in the other by induction, the result being that the vibrations are raised and the person polarizes toward the Positive end of the scale instead toward the Negative, and his Fear and other negative emotions are transmuted to Courage and similar positive mental states. A little study will show you that these mental changes are nearly all along the line of Polarization, the change being one of degree rather than of kind.

A knowledge of the existence of this great Hermetic Principle will enable the student to better understand his own mental states, and those of other people. He will see that these states are all matters of degree, and seeing thus, he will be able to raise or lower the vibration at will--to change his mental poles, and thus be Master of his mental states, instead of being their servant and slave. And by his knowledge he will be able to aid his fellows intelligently and by the appropriate methods change the polarity when the same is desirable. We advise all students to familiarize themselves with this Principle of Polarity, for a correct understanding of the same will throw light on many difficult subjects.

CHAPTER XI

RHYTHM

"Everything flows out and in; everything has its tides; all things rise and fall; the pendulum-swing manifests in everything; the measure of the swing to the right, is the measure of the swing to the left; rhythm compensates"--The Kybalion.

The great Fifth Hermetic Principle--the Principle of Rhythm- embodies the truth that in everything there is manifested a measured motion; a to-and-from movement; a flow and inflow; a swing forward and backward; a pendulum-like movement; a tide-like ebb and flow; a high-tide and a low- tide; between the two-poles manifest on the physical, mental or spiritual planes. The Principle of rhythm is closely connected with the Principle of Polarity described in the preceding chapter. Rhythm manifests between the two poles established by the Principle of Polarity. This does not mean, however, that the pendulum of Rhythm swings to the extreme poles, for this rarely happens; in fact, it is difficult to establish the extreme polar opposites in the majority of cases. But the swing is ever "toward" first one pole and then the other.

There is always an action and reaction; an advance and a retreat; a rising and a sinking; manifested in all of the airs and phenomena of the Universe. Suns, worlds, men, animals, plants, minerals, forces, energy, mind and matter, yes, even Spirit, manifests this Principle. The Principle manifests in the creation and destruction of worlds; in the rise and fall of nations; in the life history of all things; and finally in the mental states of Man.

Beginning with the manifestations of Spirit--of THE ALL--it will be noticed that there is ever the Outpouring and the Indrawing; the "Outbreathing and Inbreathing of Brahm," as the Brahmans word it. Universes are created; reach their extreme low point of

Rhythm

materiality; and then begin in their upward swing. Suns spring into being, and then their height of power being reached, the process of retrogression begins, and after aeons they become dead masses of matter, awaiting another impulse which starts again their inner energies into activity and a new solar life cycle is begun. And thus it is with all the worlds; they are born, grow and die; only to be reborn. And thus it is with all the things of shape and form; they swing from action to reaction; from birth to death; from activity to inactivity--and then back again. Thus it is with all living things; they are born, grow, and die--and then are reborn. So it is with all great movements, philosophies, creeds, fashions, governments, nations, and all else-birth, growth, maturity, decadence, death-and then new-birth. The swing of the pendulum is ever in evidence.

Night follows day; and day night. The pendulum swings from Summer to Winter, and then back again. The corpuscles, atoms, molecules, and all masses of matter, swing around the circle of their nature. There is no such thing as absolute rest, or cessation from movement, and all movement partakes of rhythm. The principle is of universal application. It may be applied to any question, or phenomena of any of the many planes of life. It may be applied to all phases of human activity. There is always the Rhythmic swing from one pole to the other. The Universal Pendulum is ever in motion. The Tides of Life flow in and out, according to Law.

The Principle of rhythm is well understood by modern science, and is considered a universal law as applied to material things. But the Hermetists carry the principle much further, and know that its manifestations and influence extend to the mental activities of Man, and that it accounts for the bewildering succession of moods, feelings and other annoying and perplexing changes that we notice in ourselves. But the Hermetists by studying the operations of this

Principle have learned to escape some of its activities by Transmutation.

The Hermetic Masters long since discovered that while the Principle of Rhythm was invariable, and ever in evidence in mental phenomena, still there were two planes of its manifestation so far as mental phenomena are concerned. They discovered that there were two general planes of Consciousness, the Lower and the Higher, the understanding of which fact enabled them to rise to the higher plane and thus escape the swing of the Rhythmic pendulum which manifested on the lower plane. In other words, the swing of the pendulum occurred on the Unconscious Plane, and the Consciousness was not affected. This they call the Law of Neutralization. Its operations consist in the raising of the Ego above the vibrations of the Unconscious Plane of mental activity, so that the negative-swing of the pendulum is not manifested in consciousness, and therefore they are not affected. It is akin to rising above a thing and letting it pass beneath you. The Hermetic Master, or advanced student, polarizes himself at the desired pole, and by a process akin to "refusing" to participate in the backward swing or, if you prefer, a "denial" of its influence over him, he stands firm in his polarized position, and allows the mental pendulum to swing back along the unconscious plane. All individuals who have attained any degree of self-mastery, accomplish this, more or less unknowingly, and by refusing to allow their moods and negative mental states to affect them, they apply the Law of Neutralization. The Master, however, carries this to a much higher degree of proficiency, and by the use of his Will he attains a degree of Poise and Mental Firmness almost impossible of belief on the part of those who allow themselves to be swung backward and forward by the mental pendulum of moods and feelings.

Rhythm

The importance of this will be appreciated by any thinking person who realizes what creatures of moods, feelings and emotion the majority of people are, and how little mastery of themselves they manifest. If you will stop and consider a moment, you will realize how much these swings of Rhythm have affected you in your life--how a period of Enthusiasm has been invariably followed by an opposite feeling and mood of Depression. Likewise, your moods and periods of Courage have been succeeded by equal moods of Fear. And so it has ever been with the majority of persons--tides of feeling have ever risen and fallen with them, but they have never suspected the cause or reason of the mental phenomena. An understanding of the workings of this Principle will give one the key to the Mastery of these rhythmic swings of feeling, and will enable him to know himself better and to avoid being carried away by these inflows and outflows. The Will is superior to the conscious manifestation of this Principle, although the Principle itself can never be destroyed. We may escape its effects, but the Principle operates, nevertheless. The pendulum ever swings, although we may escape being carried along with it.

There are other features of the operation of this Principle of Rhythm of which we wish to speak at this point. There comes into its operations that which is known as the Law of Compensation. One of the definitions or meanings of the word "Compensate" is, "to counterbalance" which is the sense in which the Hermetists use the term. It is this Law of Compensation to which the Kybalion refers when it says: "The measure of the swing to the right is the measure of the swing to the left; rhythm compensates."

The Law of Compensation is that the swing in one direction determines the swing in the opposite direction, or to the opposite pole-the one balances, or counterbalances, the other. On the Physical Plane we see many examples of this Law. The pendulum of the clock swings a certain distance to the right, and then an equal distance to the left. The seasons balance each other in the same way. The tides follow the same Law. And the same Law is manifested in all the phenomena of Rhythm. The pendulum, with a short swing in one direction, has but a short swing in the other; while the long swing to the right invariably means the long swing to the left. An object hurled upward to a certain height has an equal distance to traverse on its return. The force with which a projectile is sent upward a mile is reproduced when the projectile returns to the earth on its return journey. This Law is constant on the Physical Plane, as reference to the standard authorities will show you.

But the Hermetists carry it still further. They teach that a man's mental states are subject to the same Law. The man who enjoys keenly, is subject to keen suffering; while he who feels but little pain is capable of feeling but little joy. The pig suffers but little mentally, and enjoys but little--he is compensated. And on the other hand, there are other animals who enjoy keenly, but whose nervous organism and temperament cause them to suffer exquisite degrees of pain and so it is with Man. There are temperaments which permit of but low degrees of enjoyment, and equally low degrees of suffering; while there are others which permit the most intense enjoyment, but also the most intense suffering. The rule is that the capacity for pain and pleasure, in each individual, are balanced. The Law of Compensation is in full operation here.

But the Hermetists go still further in this matter. They teach that before one is able to enjoy a certain degree of pleasure, he must have swung as far, proportionately, toward the other pole of feeling. They hold, however, that the Negative is precedent to the Positive in this matter, that is to say that in experiencing a certain degree of pleasure it does not follow that he will have to "pay up for it" with a corresponding degree of pain; on the contrary, the pleasure is the Rhythmic swing, according to the Law of Compensation, for a degree of pain previously experienced either

Rhythm

in the present life, or in a previous incarnation. This throws a new light on the Problem of Pain.

The Hermetists regard the chain of lives as continuous, and as forming a part of one life of the individual, so that in consequence the rhythmic swing is understood in this way, while it would be without meaning unless the truth of reincarnation is admitted.

But the Hermetists claim that the Master or advanced student is able, to a great degree, to escape the swing toward Pain, by the process of Neutralization before mentioned. By rising on to the higher plane of the Ego, much of the experience that comes to those dwelling on the lower plane is avoided and escaped.

The Law of Compensation plays an important part in the lives of men and women. It will be noticed that one generally "pays the price" of anything he possesses or lacks. If he has one thing, he lacks another--the balance is struck. No one can "keep his penny and have the bit of cake" at the same time Everything has its pleasant and unpleasant sides. The things that one gains are always paid for by the things that one loses. The rich possess much that the poor lack, while the poor often possess things that are beyond the reach of the rich. The millionaire may have the inclination toward feasting, and the wealth wherewith to secure all the dainties and luxuries of the table, while he lacks the appetite to enjoy the same; he envies the appetite and digestion of the laborer who lacks the wealth and inclinations of the millionaire, and who gets more pleasure from his plain food than the millionaire could obtain even if his appetite were not jaded, nor his digestion ruined, for the wants, habits and inclinations differ. And so it is through life. The Law of Compensation is ever in operation, striving to balance and counter-balance, and always succeeding in time, even though several lives may be required for the return swing of the Pendulum of Rhythm.

The Kybalion

CHAPTER XII

CAUSATION

"Every Cause has its Effect; every Effect has its Cause; everything happens according to Law; Chance is but a name for Law not recognized; there are many planes of causation, but nothing escapes the Law."--The Kybalion.

The great Sixth Hermetic Principle--the Principle of Cause and Effect--embodies the truth that Law pervades the Universe; that nothing happens by Chance; that Chance is merely a term indicating cause existing but not recognized or perceived; that phenomena is continuous, without break or exception.

The Principle of Cause and Effect underlies all scientific thought, ancient and modern, and was enunciated by the Hermetic Teachers in the earliest days. While many and varied disputes between the many schools of thought have since arisen, these disputes have been principally upon the details of the operations of the Principle, and still more often upon the meaning of certain words. The underlying Principle of Cause and Effect has been accepted as correct by practically all the thinkers of the world worthy of the name. To think otherwise would be to take the phenomena of the universe from the domain of Law and Order, and to relegate it; to the control of the imaginary something which men have called "Chance."

A little consideration will show anyone that there is in reality no such thing as pure chance. Webster defines the word "Chance" as follows: "A supposed agent or mode of activity other than a force, law or purpose; the operation or activity of such agent; the supposed effect of such an agent; a happening; fortuity; casualty, etc." But a little consideration will show you that there can be no such agent as "Chance," in the sense of something outside of Law-something outside of Cause and Effect. How could there be a something acting in the phenomenal universe, independent of the laws, order, and continuity of the latter? Such a something would be entirely independent of the orderly trend of the universe, and therefore superior to it. We can imagine nothing outside of THE ALL being outside of the Law, and that only because THE ALL is the LAW in itself. There is no room in the universe for a something outside of and independent of Law. The existence of such a Something would render all Natural Laws ineffective, and would plunge the universe into chaotic disorder and lawlessness.

A careful examination will show that what we call "Chance" is merely an expression relating to obscure causes; causes that we cannot perceive; causes that we cannot understand. The word Chance is derived from a word Meaning "to fall" (as the falling of dice), the idea being that the fall of the dice (and many other happenings) are merely a "happening" unrelated to any cause. And this is the sense in which the term is generally employed. But when the matter is closely examined, it is seen that there is no chance whatsoever about the fall of the dice. Each time a die falls, and displays a certain number, it obeys a law as infallible as that which governs the revolution of the planets around the sun. Back of the fall of the die are causes, or chains of causes, running back further than the mind can follow. The position of the die in the box; the amount of muscular energy expended in the throw; the condition of the table, etc., etc., all are causes, the effect of which may be seen. But back of these seen causes there are chains of unseen preceding causes, all of which had a bearing upon the number of the die which fell uppermost.

If a die be cast a great number of times, it will be found that the numbers shown will be about equal, that is, there will be an equal number of one-spot, two-spot, etc., coming uppermost. Toss a penny in the air, and it may come down either "heads" or "tails";

Causation

but make a sufficient number of tosses, and the heads and tails will about even up. This is the operation of the law of average. But both the average and the single toss come under the Law of Cause and Effect, and if we were able to examine into the preceding causes, it would be clearly seen that it was simply impossible for the die to fall other than it did, under the same circumstances and at the same time. Given the same causes, the same results will follow. There is always a "cause" and a "because" to every event. Nothing ever "happens" without a cause, or rather a chain of causes.

Some confusion has arisen in the minds of persons considering this Principle, from the fact that they were unable to explain how one thing could cause another thing--that is, be the "creator" of the second thing. As a matter of fact, no "thing" ever causes or "creates" another "thing." Cause and Effect deals merely with "events." An "event" is "that which comes, arrives or happens, as a result or consequent of some preceding event." No event "creates" another event, but is merely a preceding link in the great orderly chain of events flowing from the creative energy of THE ALL. There is a continuity between all events precedent, consequent and subsequent. There is a relation existing between everything that has gone before, and everything that follows. A stone is dislodged from a mountain side and crashes through a roof of a cottage in the valley below. At first sight we regard this as a chance effect, but when we examine the matter we find a great chain of causes behind it. In the first place there was the rain which softened the earth supporting the stone and which allowed it to fall; then back of that was the influence of the sun, other rains, etc., which gradually disintegrated the piece of rock from a larger piece; then there were the causes which led to the formation of the mountain, and its upheaval by convulsions of nature, and so on ad infinitum. Then we might follow up the causes behind the rain, etc. Then we might consider the existence of the roof In short, we would soon find ourselves involved in a mesh of cause and effect, from which we would soon strive to extricate ourselves.

Just as a man has two parents, and four grandparents, and eight great-grandparents, and sixteen great-great-grandparents, and so on until when, say, forty generations are calculated the numbers of ancestors run into many millions--so it is with the number of causes behind even the most trifling event or phenomena, such as the passage of a tiny speck of soot before your eye. It is not an easy matter to trace the bit of soot hack to the early period of the world's history when it formed a part of a massive tree-trunk, which was afterward converted into coal, and so on, until as the speck of soot it now passes before your vision on its way to other adventures. And a mighty chain of events, causes and effects, brought it to its present condition, and the later is but one of the chain of events which will go to produce other events hundreds of years from now. One of the series of events arising from the tiny bit of soot was the writing of these lines, which caused the typesetter to perform certain work; the proofreader to do likewise; and which will arouse certain thoughts in your mind, and that of others, which in turn will affect others, and so on, and on, and on, beyond the ability of man to think further-and all from the passage of a tiny bit of soot, all of which shows the relativity and association of things, and the further fact that "there is no great; there is no small, in the mind that causeth all."

Stop to think a moment. If a certain man had not met a certain maid, away back in the dim period of the Stone Age--you who are now reading these lines would not now be here. And if, perhaps, the same couple had failed to meet, we who now write these lines would not now be here. And the very act of writing, on our part, and the act of reading, on yours, will affect not only the respective lives of yourself and ourselves, but will also have a direct, or indirect, affect upon many other people now living and who will

Causation

live in the ages to come. Every thought we think, every act we perform, has its direct and indirect results which fit into the great chain of Cause and Effect.

We do not wish to enter into a consideration of Free Will, or Determinism, in this work, for various reasons. Among the many reasons, is the principal one that neither side of the controversy is entirely right-in fact, both sides are partially right, according to the Hermetic Teachings. The Principle of Polarity shows that both are but Half-Truths the opposing poles of Truth. The Teachings are that a man may be both Free and yet bound by Necessity, depending upon the meaning of the terms, and the height of Truth from which the matter is examined. The ancient writers express the matter thus: "The further the creation is from the Centre, the more it is bound; the nearer the Centre it reaches, the nearer Free is it."

The majority of people are more or less the slaves of heredity, environment, etc., and manifest very little Freedom. They are swayed by the opinions, customs and thoughts of the outside world, and also by their emotions, feelings, moods, etc. They manifest no Mastery, worthy of the name. They indignantly repudiate this assertion, saying, "Why, I certainly am free to act and do as I please--I do just what I want to do," but they fail to explain whence arise the "want to" and "as I please." What makes them "want to" do one thing in preference to another; what makes them "please" to do this, and not do that? Is there no "because" to their "pleasing" and "Wanting"? The Master can change these "pleases" and "wants" into others at the opposite end of the mental pole. He is able to "Will to will," instead of to will because some feeling, mood, emotion, or environmental suggestion arouses a tendency or desire within him so to do.

The majority of people are carried along like the falling stone, obedient to environment, outside influences and internal moods,

The Kybalion

desires, etc., not to speak of the desires and wills of others stronger than themselves, heredity, environment, and suggestion, carrying them along without resistance on their part, or the exercise of the Will. Moved like the pawns on the checkerboard of life, they play their parts and are laid aside after the game is over. But the Masters, knowing the rules of the game, rise above the plane of material life, and placing themselves in touch with the higher powers of their nature, dominate their own moods, characters, qualities, and polarity, as well as the environment surrounding them and thus become Movers in the game, instead of Pawns-Causes instead of Effects. The Masters do not escape the Causation of the higher planes, but fall in with the higher laws, and thus master circumstances on the lower plane. They thus form a conscious part of the Law, instead of being mere blind instruments. While they Serve on the Higher Planes, they Rule on the Material Plane.

But, on higher and on lower, the Law is always in operation. There is no such thing as Chance. The blind goddess has been abolished by Reason. We are able to see now, with eyes made clear by knowledge, that everything is governed by Universal Law-that the infinite number of laws are but manifestations of the One Great Law-the LAW which is THE ALL. It is true indeed that not a sparrow drops unnoticed by the Mind of THE AL--that even the hairs on our head are numbered--as the scriptures have said There is nothing outside of Law; nothing that happens contrary to it. And yet, do not make the mistake of supposing that Man is but a blind automaton-far from that. The Hermetic Teachings are that Man may use Law to overcome laws, and that the higher will always prevail against the lower, until at last he has reached the stage in which he seeks refuge in the LAW itself, and laughs the phenomenal laws to scorn. Are you able to grasp the inner meaning of this?

CHAPTER XIII

GENDER

"Gender is in everything; everything has its Masculine and Feminine Principles; Gender manifests on all planes."--The Kybalion.

The great Seventh Hermetic Principle--the Principle of Gender--embodies the truth that there is Gender manifested in everything--that the Masculine and Feminine principles are ever present and active in all phases of phenomena, on each and every plane of life. At this point we think it well to call your attention to the fact that Gender, in its Hermetic sense, and Sex in the ordinarily accepted use of the term, are not the same.

The word "Gender" is derived from the Latin root meaning "to beget; to procreate; to generate; to create; to produce." A moment's consideration will show you that the word has a much broader and more general meaning than the term "Sex," the latter referring to the physical distinctions between male and female living things. Sex is merely a manifestation of Gender on a certain plane of the Great Physical Plane--the plane of organic life. We wish to impress this distinction upon your minds, for the reason that certain writers, who have acquired a smattering of the Hermetic Philosophy, have sought to identify this Seventh Hermetic Principle with wild and fanciful, and often reprehensible, theories and teachings regarding Sex.

The office of Gender is solely that of creating, producing, generating, etc., and its manifestations are visible on every plane of phenomena. It is somewhat difficult to produce proofs of this along scientific lines, for the reason that science has not as yet recognized this Principle as of universal application. But still some proofs are forthcoming from scientific sources. In the first place, we find a distinct manifestation of the Principle of Gender among the corpuscles, ions, or electrons, which constitute the basis of Matter as science now knows the latter, and which by forming certain combinations form the Atom, which until lately was regarded as final and indivisible.

The latest word of science is that the atom is composed of a multitude of corpuscles, electrons, or ions (the various names being applied by different authorities) revolving around each other and vibrating at a high degree and intensity. But the accompanying statement is made that the formation of the atom is really due to the clustering of negative corpuscles around a positive one---the positive corpuscles seeming to exert a certain influence upon the negative corpuscles, causing the latter to assume certain combinations and thus "create" or "generate" an atom. This is in line with the most ancient Hermetic Teachings, which have always identified the Masculine principle of Gender with the "Positive," and the Feminine with the "Negative" Poles of Electricity (so called).

Now a word at this point regarding this identification. The public mind has formed an entirely erroneous impression regarding the qualities of the so-called "Negative" pole of electrified or magnetized Matter. The terms Positive and Negative are very wrongly applied to this phenomenon by science. The word Positive means something real and strong, as compared with a Negative unreality or weakness. Nothing is further from the real facts of electrical phenomenon. The so-called Negative pole of the battery is really the pole in and by which the generation or production of new forms and energies is manifested. There is nothing "negative" about it. The best scientific authorities now use the word "Cathode" in place of "Negative," the word Cathode coming from the Greek root meaning "descent; the path of generation, etc," From the Cathode pole emerge the swarm of electrons or corpuscles; from the same pole emerge those wonderful "rays" which have revolutionized scientific conceptions during the past decade. The Cathode pole is the Mother of all of the strange phenomena which have rendered useless the old textbooks, and which have caused many long accepted theories to be relegated to the scrap-pile of scientific speculation. The Cathode, or Negative Pole, is the Mother Principle of Electrical Phenomena, and of the finest forms of matter as yet known to science. So you see we are justified in refusing to use the term "Negative" in our consideration of the subject, and in insisting upon substituting the word "Feminine" for the old term. The facts of the case bear us out in this, without taking the Hermetic Teachings into consideration. And so we shall use the word "Feminine" in the place of "Negative" in speaking of that pole of activity.

The latest scientific teachings are that the creative corpuscles or electrons are Feminine (science says "they are composed of negative electricity"-we say they are composed of Feminine energy). A Feminine corpuscle becomes detached from, or rather leaves, a Masculine corpuscle, and starts on a new career. It actively seeks a union with a Masculine corpuscle, being urged thereto by the natural impulse to create new forms of Matter or Energy. One writer goes so far as to use the term "it at once seeks, of its own volition, a union," etc. This detachment and uniting form the basis of the greater part of the activities of the chemical world. When the Feminine corpuscle unites with a Masculine corpuscle, a certain process is begun. The Feminine particles vibrate rapidly under the influence of the Masculine energy, and circle rapidly around the latter. The result is the birth of a new atom. This new atom is really composed of a union of the Masculine and Feminine electrons, or corpuscles, but when the union is formed the atom is a separate thing, having certain properties, but no longer manifesting the property of free electricity. The process of detachment or separation of the Feminine electrons is called "ionization." These electrons, or corpuscles, are the most active workers in Nature's field. Arising from their unions, or combinations, manifest the varied phenomena of light, heat, electricity, magnetism, attraction, repulsion, chemical affinity and the reverse, and similar phenomena. And all this arises from the operation of the Principle of Gender on the plane of Energy.

The part of the Masculine principle seems to be that of directing a certain inherent energy toward the Feminine principle, and thus starting into activity the creative processes. But the Feminine principle is the one always doing the active creative work-and this is so on all planes. And yet, each principle is incapable of operative energy without the assistance of the other. In some of the forms of life, the two principles are combined in one organism. For that matter, everything in the organic world manifests both genders-- there is always the Masculine present in the Feminine form, and the Feminine form. The Hermetic Teachings include much regarding the operation of the two principles of Gender in the production and manifestation of various forms of energy, etc., but we do not deem it expedient to go into detail regarding the same at this point, because we are unable to back up the same with scientific proof, for the reason that science has not as yet progressed thus far. But the example we have given you of the phenomena of the electrons or corpuscles will show you that science is on the right path, and will also give you a general idea of the underlying principles.

Some leading scientific investigators have announced their belief that in the formation of crystals there was to be found something that corresponded to "sex-activity" which is another straw showing the direction the scientific winds are blowing. And each year will bring other facts to corroborate the correctness of the Hermetic Principle of Gender. It will be found that Gender is in

Gender

constant operation and manifestation in the field of inorganic matter, and in the field of Energy or Force. Electricity is now generally regarded as the "Something" into which all other forms of energy seem to melt or dissolve. The "Electrical Theory of the Universe" is the latest scientific doctrine, and is growing rapidly in popularity and general acceptance. And it thus follows that if we are able to discover in the phenomena of electricity-even at the very root and source of its manifestations a clear and unmistakable evidence of the presence of Gender and its activities, we are justified in asking you to believe that science at last has offered proofs of the existence in all universal phenomena of that great Hermetic Principle-the Principle of Gender.

It is not necessary to take up your time with the well known phenomena of the "attraction and repulsion" of the atoms; chemical affinity; the "loves and hates" of the atomic particles; the attraction or cohesion between the molecules of matter. These facts are too well known to need extended comment from us. But, have you ever considered that all of these things are manifestations of the Gender Principle? Can you not see that the phenomena is "on all fours" with that of the corpuscles or electrons? And more than this, can you not see the reasonableness of the Hermetic Teachings which assert that the very Law of Gravitation-that strange attraction by reason of which all particles and bodies of matter in the universe tend toward each other is but another manifestation of the Principle of Gender, which operates in the direction of attracting the Masculine to the Feminine energies, and vice versa? We cannot offer you scientific proof of this at this time-but examine the phenomena in the light of the Hermetic Teachings on the subject, and see if you have not a better working hypothesis than any offered by physical science. Submit all physical phenomena to the test, and you will discern the Principle of Gender ever in evidence.

Let us now pass on to a consideration of the operation of the Principle on the Mental Plane. Many interesting features are there awaiting examination.

CHAPTER XIV

MENTAL GENDER

Students of psychology who have followed the modern trend of thought along the lines of mental phenomena are struck by the persistence of the dual-mind idea which has manifested itself so strongly during the past ten or fifteen years, and which has given rise to a number of plausible theories regarding the nature and constitution of these "two minds." The late Thomson J. Hudson attained great popularity in 1893 by advancing his well-known theory of the "objective and subjective minds" which he held existed in every individual. Other writers have attracted almost equal attention by the theories regarding the "conscious and subconscious minds"; the "voluntary and involuntary minds"; "the active and passive minds," etc., etc. The theories of the various writers differ from each other, but there remains the underlying principle of "the duality of mind."

The student of the Hermetic Philosophy is tempted to smile when he reads and hears of these many "new theories" regarding the duality of mind, each school adhering tenaciously to its own pet theories, and each claiming to have "discovered the truth." The student turns back the pages of occult history, and away back in the dim beginnings of occult teachings he finds references to the ancient Hermetic doctrine of the Principle of Gender on the Mental Plane-the manifestation of Mental Gender. And examining further he finds that the ancient philosophy took cognizance of the phenomenon of the "dual mind," and accounted for it by the theory of Mental Gender. This idea of Mental Gender may be explained in a few words to students who are familiar with the modern theories just alluded to. The Masculine Principle of Mind corresponds to the so-called Objective Mind; Conscious Mind; Voluntary Mind; Active Mind, etc. And the Feminine Principle of

Mind corresponds to the so-called Subjective Mind; Sub-conscious Mind; Involuntary Mind; Passive Mind, etc. Of course the Hermetic Teachings do not agree with the many modern theories regarding the nature of the two phases of mind, nor does it admit many of the facts claimed for the two respective aspects--some of the said theories and claims being very far-fetched and incapable of standing the test of experiment and demonstration. We point to the phases of agreement merely for the purpose of helping the student to assimilate his previously acquired knowledge with the teachings of the Hermetic Philosophy. Students of Hudson will notice the statement at the beginning of his second chapter of "The Law of Psychic Phenomena," that: "The mystic jargon of the Hermetic philosophers discloses the same general idea" i.e., the duality of mind. If Dr. Hudson had taken the time and trouble to decipher a little of "the mystic jargon of the Hermetic Philosophy," he might have received much light upon the subject of "the dual mind"--but then, perhaps, his most interesting work might not have been written. Let us now consider the Hermetic Teachings regarding Mental Gender.

The Hermetic Teachers impart their instruction regarding this subject by bidding their students examine the report of their consciousness regarding their Self. The students are bidden to turn their attention inward upon the Self dwelling within each. Each student is led to see that his consciousness gives him first a report of the existence of his Self-the report is "I Am." This at first seems to be the final words from the consciousness, but a little further examination discloses the fact that this "I Am" may be separated or split into two distinct parts, or aspects, which while working in unison and in conjunction, yet, nevertheless, may be separated in consciousness.

While at first there seems to be only an "I" existing, a more careful and closer examination reveals the fact that there exists an "I" and

Mental Gender

a "Me." These mental twins differ in their characteristics and nature, and an examination of their nature and the phenomena arising from the same will throw much light upon many of the problems of mental influence.

Let us begin with a consideration of the Me, which is usually mistaken for the I by the student, until he presses the inquiry a little further back into the recesses of consciousness. A man thinks of his Self (in its aspect of Me) as being composed of certain feelings, tastes likes, dislikes, habits, peculiar ties, characteristics, etc., all of which go to make up his personality, or the "Self" known to himself and others. He knows that these emotions and feelings change; are born and die away; are subject to the Principle of Rhythm, and the Principle of Polarity, which take him from one extreme of feeling to another. He also thinks of the "Me" as being certain knowledge gathered together in his mind, and thus forming a part of himself. This is the "Me" of a man.

But we have proceeded too hastily. The "Me" of many men may be said to consist largely of their consciousness of the body and their physical appetites, etc. Their consciousness being largely bound up with their bodily nature, they practically "live there." Some men even go so far as to regard their personal apparel as a part of their "Me" and actually seem to consider it a part of themselves. A writer has humorously said that "men consist of three parts--soul, body and clothes." These "clothes conscious" people would lose their personality if divested of their clothing by savages upon the occasion of a shipwreck. But even many who are not so closely bound up with the idea of personal raiment stick closely to the consciousness of their bodies being their "Me" They cannot conceive of a Self independent of the body. Their mind seems to them to be practically "a something belonging to" their body-which in many cases it is indeed.

The Kybalion

But as man rises in the scale of consciousness he is able to disentangle his "Me" from his idea of body, and is able to think of his body as "belonging to" the mental part of him. But even then he is very apt to identify the "Me" entirely with the mental states, feelings, etc., which he feels to exist within him. He is very apt to consider these internal states as identical with himself, instead of their being simply "things" produced by some part of his mentality, and existing within him--of him, and in him, but still not "himself." He sees that he may change these internal states of feelings by all effort of will, and that he may produce a feeling or state of an exactly opposite nature, in the same way, and yet the same "Me" exists. And so after a while he is able to set aside these various mental states, emotions, feelings, habits, qualities, characteristics, and other personal mental belongings--he is able to set them aside in the "not-me" collection of curiosities and encumbrances, as well as valuable possessions. This requires much mental concentration and power of mental analysis on the part of the student. But still the task is possible for the advanced student, and even those not so far advanced are able to see, in the imagination, how the process may be performed.

After this laying-aside process has been performed, the student will find himself in conscious possession of a "Self" which may be considered in its "I" and "Me" dual aspects. The "Me" will be felt to be a Something mental in which thoughts, ideas, emotions, feelings, and other mental states may be produced. It may be considered as the "mental womb," as the ancients styled it-capable of generating mental offspring. It reports to the consciousness as a "Me" with latent powers of creation and generation of mental progeny of all sorts and kinds. Its powers of creative energy are felt to be enormous. But still it seems to be conscious that it must receive some form of energy from either its "I" companion, or else from some other "I" ere it is able to bring into being its mental

Mental Gender

creations. This consciousness brings with it a realization of an enormous capacity for mental work and creative ability.

But the student soon finds that this is not all that he finds within his inner consciousness. He finds that there exists a mental Something which is able to Will that the "Me" act along certain creative lines, and which is also able to stand aside and witness the mental creation. This part of himself he is taught to call his "I." He is able to rest in its consciousness at will. He finds there not a consciousness of an ability to generate and actively create, in the sense of the gradual process attendant upon mental operations, but rather a sense and consciousness of an ability to project an energy from the "I" to the "Me"--a process of "willing" that the mental creation begin and proceed. He also finds that the "I" is able to stand aside and witness the operations of the "Me's" mental creation and generation. There is this dual aspect in the mind of every person. The "I" represents the Masculine Principle of Mental Gender-the "Me" represents the Female Principle. The "I" represents the Aspect of Being; the "Me" the Aspect of Becoming. You will notice that the Principle of Correspondence operates on this plane just as it does upon the great plane upon which the creation of Universes is performed. The two are similar in kind, although vastly different in degree. "As above, so below; as below, so above."

These aspects of mind-the Masculine and Feminine Principles-the "I" and the "Me"-considered in connection with the well-known mental and psychic phenomena, give the master-key to these dimly known regions of mental operation and manifestation. The principle of Mental Gender gives the truth underlying the whole field of the phenomena of mental influence, etc.

The tendency of the Feminine Principle is always in the direction of receiving impressions, while the tendency of the Masculine Principle is always in the direction of giving, out or expressing.

The Kybalion

The Feminine Principle has much more varied field of operation than has the Masculine Principle. The Feminine Principle conducts the work of generating new thoughts, concepts, ideas, including the work of the imagination. The Masculine Principle contents itself with the work of the "Will" in its varied phases. And yet, without the active aid of the Will of the Masculine Principle, the Feminine Principle is apt to rest content with generating mental images which are the result of impressions received from outside, instead of producing original mental creations.

Persons who can give continued attention and thought to a subject actively employ both of the Mental Principles-the Feminine in the work of the mental generation, and the Masculine Will in stimulating and energizing the creative portion of the mind. The majority of persons really employ the Masculine Principle but little, and are content to live according to the thoughts and ideas instilled into the "Me" from the "I" of other minds. But it is not our purpose to dwell upon this phase of the subject, which may be studied from any good text-book upon psychology, with the key that we have given you regarding Mental Gender.

The student of Psychic Phenomena is aware of the wonderful phenomena classified under the head of Telepathy; Thought Transference; Mental Influence; Suggestion; Hypnotism, etc. Many have sought for an explanation of these varied phases of phenomena under the theories of the various "dual mind" teachers. And in a measure they are right, for there is clearly a manifestation of two distinct phases of mental activity. But if such students will consider these "dual minds" in the light of the Hermetic Teachings regarding Vibrations and Mental Gender, they will see that the long sought for key is at hand.

In the phenomena of Telepathy it is seen how the Vibratory Energy of the Masculine Principle is projected toward the Feminine Principle of another person, and the latter takes the seed-thought

Mental Gender

and allows it to develop into maturity. In the same way Suggestion and Hypnotism operates. The Masculine Principle of the person giving the suggestions directs a stream of Vibratory Energy or Will-Power toward the Feminine Principle of the other person, and the latter accepting it makes it its own and acts and thinks accordingly. An idea thus lodged in the mind of another person grows and develops, and in time is regarded as the rightful mental offspring of the individual, whereas it is in reality like the cuckoo egg placed in the sparrows nest, where it destroys the rightful offspring and makes itself at home. The normal method is for the Masculine and Feminine Principles in a person's mind to coordinate and act harmoniously in conjunction with each other, but, unfortunately, the Masculine Principle in the average person is too lazy to act-the display of Will-Power is too slight-and the consequence is that such persons are ruled almost entirely by the minds and wills of other persons, whom they allow to do their thinking and willing for them. How few original thoughts or original actions are performed by the average person? Are not the majority of persons mere shadows and echoes of others having stronger wills or minds than themselves? The trouble is that the average person dwells almost altogether in his "Me" consciousness and does not realize that he has such a thing as an "I." He is polarized in his Feminine Principle of Mind, and the Masculine Principle, in which is lodged the Will, is allowed to remain inactive and not employed.

The strong men and women of the world invariably manifest the Masculine Principle of Will, and their strength depends materially upon this fact. Instead of living upon the impressions made upon their minds by others, they dominate their own minds by their Will, obtaining the kind of mental images desired, and moreover dominate the minds of others likewise, in the same manner. Look at the strong people, how they manage to implant their seed-thoughts in the minds of the masses of the people, thus causing the latter to think thoughts in accordance with the desires and wills of the strong individuals. This is why the masses of people are such sheeplike creatures, never originating an idea of their own, nor using their own powers of mental activity.

The manifestation of Mental Gender may be noticed all around us in everyday life. The magnetic persons are those who are able to use the Masculine Principle in the way of impressing their ideas upon others. The actor who makes people weep or cry as he wills, is employing this principle. And so is the successful orator, statesman, preacher, writer or other people who are before the public attention. The peculiar influence exerted by some people over others is due to the manifestation of Mental Gender, along the Vibrational lines above indicated. In this principle lies the secret of personal magnetism, personal influence, fascination, etc., as well as the phenomena generally grouped under the name of Hypnotism.

The student who has familiarized himself with the phenomena generally spoken of as "psychic" will have discovered the important part played in the said phenomena by that force which science has styled "Suggestion," by which term is meant the process or method whereby an idea is transferred to, or "impressed upon" the mind of another, causing the second mind to act in accordance therewith. A correct understanding of Suggestion is necessary in order to intelligently comprehend the varied psychical phenomena which Suggestion underlies. But, still more is a knowledge of Vibration and Mental Gender necessary for the student of Suggestion. For the whole principle of Suggestion depends upon the principle of Mental Gender and Vibration.

It is customary for the writers and teachers of Suggestion to explain that it is the "objective or voluntary" mind which make the mental impression, or suggestion, upon the "subjective or involuntary" mind. But they do not describe the process or give us

Mental Gender

any analogy in nature whereby we may more readily comprehend the idea. But if you will think of the matter in the light of the Hermetic Teachings you will be able to see that the energizing of the Feminine Principle by the Vibratory Energy of the Masculine Principle Is in accordance to the universal laws of nature, and that the natural world affords countless analogies whereby the principle may be understood. In fact, the Hermetic Teachings show that the very creation of the Universe follows the same law, and that in all creative manifestations, upon the planes of the spiritual, the mental, and the physical, there is always in operation this principle of Gender-this manifestation of the Masculine and the Feminine Principles. "As above, so below; as below, so above." And more than this, when the principle of Mental Gender is once grasped and understood, the varied phenomena of psychology at once becomes capable of intelligent classification and study, instead of being very much in the dark. The principle "works out" in practice, because it is based upon the immutable universal laws of life.

We shall not enter into an extended discussion of, or description of, the varied phenomena of mental influence or psychic activity. There are many books, many of them quite good, which have been written and published on this subject of late years. The main facts stated in these various books are correct, although the several writers have attempted to explain the phenomena by various pet theories of their own. The student may acquaint himself with these matters, and by using the theory of Mental Gender he will be able to bring order out of the chaos of conflicting theory and teachings, and may, moreover, readily make himself a master of the subject if he be so inclined. The purpose of this work is not to give an extended account of psychic phenomena but rather to give to the student a master-key whereby He may unlock the many doors leading into the parts of the Temple of Knowledge which he may wish to explore. We feel that in this consideration of the teachings of The Kybalion, one may find an explanation which will serve to clear away many perplexing difficulties--a key that will unlock many doors. What is the use of going into detail regarding all of the many features of psychic phenomena and mental science, provided we place in the hands of the student the means whereby he may acquaint himself fully regarding any phase of the subject which may interest him. With the aid of The Kybalion one may go through any occult library anew, the old Light from Egypt illuminating many dark pages, and obscure subjects. That is the purpose of this book. We do not come expounding a new philosophy, but rather furnishing the outlines of a great world-old teaching which will make clear the teachings of others-which will serve as a Great Reconciler of differing: theories, and opposing doctrines.

CHAPTER XV

HERMETIC AXIOMS

"The possession of Knowledge, unless accompanied by a manifestation and expression in Action, is like the hoarding of precious metals-a vain and foolish thing. Knowledge, like wealth, is intended for Use. The Law of Use is Universal, and he who violates it suffers by reason of his conflict with natural forces."--The Kybalion.

The Hermetic Teachings, while always having been kept securely locked up in the minds of the fortunate possessors thereof, for reasons which we have already stated, were never intended to be merely stored away and secreted. The Law of Use is dwelt upon in the Teachings, as you may see by reference to the above quotation from The Kybalion, which states it forcibly. Knowledge without Use and Expression is a vain thing, bringing no good to its possessor, or to the race. Beware of Mental Miserliness, and express into Action that which you have learned. Study the Axioms and Aphorisms, but practice them also.

We give below some of the more important Hermetic Axioms, from The Kybalion, with a few comments added to each. Make these your own, and practice and use them, for they are not really your own until you have Used them.

"To change your mood or mental state--change your vibration."--The Kybalion.

One may change his mental vibrations by an effort of Will, in the direction of deliberately fixing the Attention upon a more desirable state. Will directs the Attention, and Attention changes the Vibration. Cultivate the Art of Attention, by means of the Will, and you have solved the secret of the Mastery of Moods and Mental States.

The Kybalion

"To destroy an undesirable rate of mental vibration, put into operation the principle of Polarity and concentrate upon the opposite pole to that which you desire to suppress. Kill out the undesirable by changing its polarity."--The Kybalion.

This is one of the most important of the Hermetic Formulas. It is based upon true scientific principles. We have shown you that a mental state and its opposite were merely the two poles of one thing, and that by Mental Transmutation the polarity might be reversed. This Principle is known to modern psychologists, who apply it to the breaking up of undesirable habits by bidding their students concentrate upon the opposite quality. If you are possessed of Fear, do not waste time trying to "kill out" Fear, but instead cultivate the quality of Courage, and the Fear will disappear. Some writers have expressed this idea most forcibly by using the illustration of the dark room. You do not have to shovel out or sweep out the Darkness, but by merely opening the shutters and letting in the Light the Darkness has disappeared. To kill out a Negative quality, concentrate upon the Positive Pole of that same quality, and the vibrations will gradually change from Negative to Positive, until finally you will become polarized on the Positive pole instead of the Negative. The reverse is also true, as many have found out to their sorrow, when they have allowed themselves to vibrate too constantly on the Negative pole of things. By changing your polarity you may master your moods, change your mental states, remake your disposition, and build up character. Much of the Mental Mastery of the advanced Hermetics is due to this application of Polarity, which is one of the important aspects of Mental Transmutation. Remember the Hermetic Axiom (quoted previously), which says:

"Mind (as well as metals and elements) may be transmuted from state to state; degree to degree, condition to condition; pole to pole; vibration to vibration."--The Kybalion.

Hermetic Axioms

The mastery of Polarization is the mastery of the fundamental principles of Mental Transmutation or Mental Alchemy, for unless one acquires the art of changing his own polarity, he will be unable to affect his environment. An understanding of this principle will enable one to change his own Polarity, as well as that of others, if he will but devote the time, care, study and practice necessary to master the art. The principle is true, but the results obtained depend upon the persistent patience and practice of the student.

"Rhythm may be neutralized by an application of the Art of Polarization."--The Kybalion.

As we have explained in previous chapters, the Hermetists hold that the Principle of Rhythm manifests on the Mental Plane as well as on the Physical Plane, and that the bewildering succession of moods, feelings, emotions, and other mental states, are due to the backward and forward swing of the mental pendulum, which carries us from one extreme of feeling to the other. The Hermetists also teach that the Law of Neutralization enables one, to a great extent, to overcome the operation of Rhythm in consciousness. As we have explained, there is a Higher Plane of Consciousness, as well as the ordinary Lower Plane, and the Master by rising mentally to the Higher Plane causes the swing of the mental pendulum to manifest on the Lower Plane, and he, dwelling on his Higher Plane, escapes the consciousness of the swing backward. This is effected by polarizing on the Higher Self, and thus raising the mental vibrations of the Ego above those of the ordinary plane of consciousness. It is akin to rising above a thing and allowing it to pass beneath you. The advanced Hermetist polarizes himself at the Positive Pole of his Being-the "I Am" pole rather than the pole of personality and by "refusing" and "denying" the operation of Rhythm, raises himself above its plane of consciousness, and standing firm in his Statement of Being he allows the pendulum to swing back on the Lower Plane without changing his Polarity. This is accomplished by all individuals who have attained any degree of self-mastery, whether they understand the law or not. Such persons simply "refuse" to allow themselves to be swung back by the pendulum of mood and emotion, and by steadfastly affirming the superiority they remain polarized on the Positive pole. The Master, of course, attains a far greater degree of proficiency, because he understands the law which he is overcoming by a higher law, and by the use of his Will he attains a degree of Poise and Mental Steadfastness almost impossible of belief on the part of those who allow themselves to be swung backward and forward by the mental pendulum of moods and feelings.

Remember always, however, that you do not really destroy the Principle of Rhythm, for that is indestructible. You simply overcome one law by counter-balancing it with another and thus maintain an equilibrium. The laws of balance and counter-balance are in operation on the mental as well as on the physical planes, and an understanding of these laws enables one to seem to overthrow laws, whereas he is merely exerting a counterbalance.

"Nothing escapes the Principle of Cause and Effect, but there are many Planes of Causation, and one may use the laws of the higher to overcome the laws of the lower."--The Kybalion.

By an understanding of the practice of Polarization, the Hermetists rise to a higher plane of Causation and thus counter-balance the laws of the lower planes of Causation. By rising above the plane of ordinary Causes they become themselves, in a degree, Causes instead of being merely Caused. By being able to master their own moods and feelings, and by being able to neutralize Rhythm, as we have already explained, they are able to escape a great part of the operations of Cause and Effect on the ordinary plane. The masses of people are carried along, obedient to their environment; the wills and desires of others stronger than themselves; the effects of inherited tendencies; the suggestions of those about them; and

Hermetic Axioms

other outward causes; which tend to move them about on the chess-board of life like mere pawns. By rising above these influencing causes, the advanced Hermetists seek a higher plane of mental action, and by dominating their moods, emotions, impulses and feelings, they create for themselves new characters, qualities and powers, by which they overcome their ordinary environment, and thus become practically players instead of mere Pawns. Such people help to play the game of life understandingly, instead of being moved about this way and that way by stronger influences and powers and wills. They use the Principle of Cause and Effect, instead of being used by it. Of course, even the highest are subject to the Principle as it manifests on the higher planes, but on the lower planes of activity, they are Masters instead of Slaves. As The Kybalion says:

"The wise ones serve on the higher, but rule on the lower. They obey the laws coming from above them, But on their own plane, and those below them they rule and give orders. And, yet, in so doing, they form a part of the Principle, instead of opposing it. The wise man falls in with the Law, and by understanding its movements he operates it instead of being its blind slave. Just as does the skilled swimmer turn this way and that way, going and coming as he will, instead of being as the log which is carried here and there--so is the wise man as compared to the ordinary man-- and yet both swimmer and log; wise man and fool, are subject to Law. He who understands this is well on the road to Mastery."--The Kybalion.

In conclusion let us again call your attention to the Hermetic Axiom:

"True Hermetic Transmutation is a Mental Art."--The Kybalion.

In the above axiom, the Hermetists teach that the great work of influencing one's environment is accomplished by Mental Power.

The Universe being wholly mental, it follows that it may be ruled only by Mentality. And in this truth is to be found an explanation of all the phenomena and manifestations of the various mental powers which are attracting so much attention and study in these earlier years of the Twentieth Century. Back of and under the teachings of the various cults and schools, remains ever constant the Principle of the Mental Substance of the Universe. If the Universe be Mental in its substantial nature, then it follows that Mental Transmutation must change the conditions and phenomena of the Universe. If the Universe is Mental, then Mind must be the highest power affecting its phenomena. If this be understood then all the so-called "miracles" and "wonder-workings" are seen plainly for what they are.

"THE ALL is MIND; The Universe is Mental."--The Kybalion.

Free Audiobook Access

Scan the QR code, input your email, and download your audiobooks!

www.ingramcontent.com/pod-product-compliance
Lightning Source LLC
Chambersburg PA
CBHW060515100426
42743CB00009B/1328